The European Union as a Global Regulator?

The European Union is often depicted as a dominant global regulator. The purpose of this volume is to move beyond establishing that the EU influences global regulation in order to identify under what conditions it exerts that influence. Toward that end, it focuses on the EU's active efforts, both bilateral and multilateral, to shape regulations beyond its borders. The empirical chapters in this volume are explicitly comparative: among foreign partners, across international contexts, over time, and across issues. The more conceptual contributions posit an explanation for the EU's choice of regulatory cooperation strategy and take stock of Market Power Europe as a dynamic conceptual framework for understanding and researching the EU as a power. Collectively, this volume advances three arguments: the utility of the EU's regulatory power resources is context specific; debates about what kind of power the EU is, at least as currently conceived, are unproductive; and that the EU's engagement in the world is better explained through general theories of international political economy.

This book was published as a special issue of the *Journal of European Public Policy*.

Alasdair R. Young is Professor of International Affairs and Jean Monnet Chair in the Sam Nunn School of International Affairs, Georgia Institute of Technology. He is also Chair of the European Union Studies Association (2015–17).

Journal of European Public Policy Series

Series Editors

Jeremy Richardson is Emeritus Fellow at Nuffield College, Oxford University, UK, and an Adjunct Professor in the National Centre for Research on Europe, University of Canterbury, New Zealand.

Berthold Rittberger is Professor and Chair of International Relations at the Geschwister-Scholl-Institute of Political Science at the University of Munich.

This series seeks to bring together some of the finest edited works on European Public Policy. Reprinting from Special Issues of the *Journal of European Public Policy*, the focus is on using a wide range of social sciences approaches, both qualitative and quantitative, to gain a comprehensive and definitive understanding of Public Policy in Europe.

Towards a Federal Europe
Edited by Alexander H. Trechsel

The Disparity of European Integration
Edited by Tanja A. Börzel

Cross-National Policy Convergence:
Causes Concepts and Empirical Findings
Edited by Christoph Knill

Civilian or Military Power?
European foreign policy in perspective
Edited by Helene Sjursen

The European Union and New Trade Politics
Edited by John Peterson and Alasdair R. Young

Comparative Studies of Policy Agendas
Edited by Frank R. Baumgartner, Christoffer Green-Pedersen and Bryan D. Jones

The Constitutionalization of the European Union
Edited by Berthold Rittberger and Frank Schimmelfenig

Empirical and Theoretical Studies in EU Lobbying
Edited by David Coen

Mutual Recognition as a New Mode of Governance
Edited by Susanne K. Schmidt

France and the European Union
Edited by Emiliano Grossman

Immigration and Integration Policy in Europe
Edited by Tim Bale

Reforming the European Commission
Edited by Michael W. Bauer
International Influence Beyond Conditionality
Postcommunist Europe after EU enlargement
Edited by Rachel A. Epstein and Ulrich Sedelmeier

The Role of Political Parties in the European Union
Edited by Björn Lindberg, Anne Rasmussen and Andreas Warntjen

EU External Governance
Projecting EU Rules beyond Membership
Edited by Sandra Lavenex and Frank Schimmelfennig

EMU and Political Science
What have we learned?
Edited by Henrik Enderlein and Amy Verdun

Learning and Governance in the EU Policy Making Process
Edited by Anthony R. Zito

Political Representation and EU Governance
Edited by Peter Mair and Jacques Thomassen

Europe and the Management of Globalization
Edited by Wade Jacoby and Sophie Meunier

Negotiation Theory and the EU
The State of the Art
Edited by Andreas Dür, Gemma Mateo and Daniel C. Thomas

The Political Economy of Europe's Incomplete Single Market
Edited by David Howarth and Tal Sadeh

The European Union's Foreign Economic Policies
A principal-agent perspective
Edited by Andreas Dür and Michael Elsig

The Politics of the Lisbon Agenda
Governance Architectures and Domestic Usages of Europe
Edited by Susana Borrás and Claudio M. Radaelli

Agency Governance in the European Union
Edited by Berthold Rittberger and Arndt Wonka

The EU Timescape
Edited by Klaus H. Goetz and Jan-Hinrik Meyer-Sahling
The EU's Common Foreign and Security Policy
Edited by Helene Sjursen

Economic Patriotism in Open Economies
Edited by Ben Clift and Cornelia Woll

The Power of the European Court of Justice
Edited by Susanne K. Schmidt and R. Daniel Kelemen

The Representative Turn in EU Studies
Edited by Sandra Kröger and Dawid Friedrich

Legislative Co-decision in the European Union
Edited by Anne Rasmussen, Charlotte Burns and Christine Reh

Frameworks of the European Union's Policy Process
Edited by Nikolaos Zahariadis

Changing Models of Capitalism in Europe and the U.S.
Edited by Richard Deeg and Gregory Jackson

Europe's Place in Global Financial Governance after the Crisis
Edited by Daniel Mügge

The European Union: Integration and Enlargement
Edited by R. Daniel Kelemen, Anand Menon and Jonathan Slapin

Coping with Power Dispersion?
Autonomy, co-ordination and control in multi-level systems
Edited by Mads Dagnis Jensen, Christel Koop and Michaël Tatham

European Democracy as Demoi-cracy
Edited by Francis Cheneval, Sandra Lavenex and Frank Schimmelfennig

Speaking with a Single Voice
The EU as an effective actor in global governance?
Edited by Eugénia da Conceição-Heldt and Sophie Meunier

European Integration in Times of Crisis
Theoretical perspectives
Edited by Demosthenes Ioannou, Patrick Leblond and Arne Niemann

Legislative Lobbying in Context
The policy and polity determinants of interest group politics in the European Union
Edited by Jan Beyers, Caelesta Braun and Heike Klüver

Differentiated Integration in the European Union
Edited by Benjamin Leruth and Christopher Lord

The European Union as a Global Regulator?
Edited by Alasdair R. Young

The European Union as a Global Regulator?

Edited by
Alasdair R. Young

LONDON AND NEW YORK

First published 2016
by Routledge
2 Park Square, Milton Park, Abingdon, Oxon, OX14 4RN, UK

and by Routledge
711 Third Avenue, New York, NY 10017, USA

Routledge is an imprint of the Taylor & Francis Group, an informa business

© 2016 Taylor & Francis

All rights reserved. No part of this book may be reprinted or reproduced or utilised in any form or by any electronic, mechanical, or other means, now known or hereafter invented, including photocopying and recording, or in any information storage or retrieval system, without permission in writing from the publishers.

Trademark notice: Product or corporate names may be trademarks or registered trademarks, and are used only for identification and explanation without intent to infringe.

British Library Cataloguing in Publication Data
A catalogue record for this book is available from the British Library

ISBN 13: 978-1-138-95138-9

Typeset in Adobe Garamond Pro
by diacriTech, Chennai

Publisher's Note
The publisher accepts responsibility for any inconsistencies that may have arisen during the conversion of this book from journal articles to book chapters, namely the possible inclusion of journal terminology.

Disclaimer
Every effort has been made to contact copyright holders for their permission to reprint material in this book. The publishers would be grateful to hear from any copyright holder who is not here acknowledged and will undertake to rectify any errors or omissions in future editions of this book.

Contents

Citation Information   xi

1. The European Union as a global regulator? Context and comparison   1
   Alasdair R. Young

2. Liberalizing trade, not exporting rules: the limits to regulatory
   co-ordination in the EU's 'new generation' preferential trade
   agreements   21
   Alasdair R. Young

3. Coercion with kid gloves? The European Union's role in shaping a global
   regulatory framework for aviation emissions   44
   Vicki L. Birchfield

4. 'Man Overboard!' Was EU influence on the Maritime Labour Convention
   lost at sea?   63
   Robert Kissack

5. Putting the EU in its place: policy strategies and the global regulatory
   context   84
   Abraham L. Newman and Elliot Posner

6. Market power Europe: exploring a dynamic conceptual framework   104
   Chad Damro

Index   123

Citation Information

The chapters in this book were originally published in the *Journal of European Public Policy*, volume 22, issue 9 (2015). When citing this material, please use the original page numbering for each article, as follows:

Chapter 1
The European Union as a global regulator? Context and comparison
Alasdair R. Young
Journal of European Public Policy, volume 22, issue 9 (2015) pp. 1233–1252

Chapter 2
Liberalizing trade, not exporting rules: the limits to regulatory co-ordination in the EU's 'new generation' preferential trade agreements
Alasdair R. Young
Journal of European Public Policy, volume 22, issue 9 (2015) pp. 1253–1275

Chapter 3
Coercion with kid gloves? The European Union's role in shaping a global regulatory framework for aviation emissions
Vicki L. Birchfield
Journal of European Public Policy, volume 22, issue 9 (2015) pp. 1276–1294

Chapter 4
'Man Overboard!' Was EU influence on the Maritime Labour Convention lost at sea?
Robert Kissack
Journal of European Public Policy, volume 22, issue 9 (2015) pp. 1295–1315

Chapter 5
Putting the EU in its place: policy strategies and the global regulatory context
Abraham L. Newman and Elliot Posner
Journal of European Public Policy, volume 22, issue 9 (2015) pp. 1316–1335

CITATION INFORMATION

Chapter 6
Market power Europe: exploring a dynamic conceptual framework
Chad Damro
Journal of European Public Policy, volume 22, issue 9 (2015) pp. 1336–1354

For any permission-related enquiries please visit
http://www.tandfonline.com/page/help/permissions

THE EUROPEAN UNION AS A GLOBAL REGULATOR?

influence by bringing together some of the papers presented at the Jean Monnet Chair (2012-3121) Workshop 'Regulatory power Europe? Assessing the EU's efforts to shape global rules' held at the Georgia Institute of Technology, 18–19 April 2014.

Supported by the three empirical contributions in the special issue, this contribution makes three main arguments. First, the EU's regulatory influence varies systematically across different forms of regulatory interaction. The utility of the EU's regulatory power resources varies in predictable ways depending on the form of regulatory interaction, whether it is regulatory competition or one of the different forms of regulatory co-operation: power-based bargaining *with* the ability to exclude others from the EU's market; power-based bargaining *without* the ability to exclude others from the EU's market; and rule-mediated negotiation. The form of regulatory interaction, therefore, is a critical variable affecting how the EU's regulatory power resources translate into influence. Second, within the different forms of regulatory co-operation the EU's influence varies in line with expectations derived from the literature. But, third, the magnitude of the EU's influence seems to be considerably less in regulatory co-operation than suggested by the literature on regulatory competition; a finding that reinforces the first argument.

The collection's three empirical contributions – on regulatory co-operation in 'new generation' preferential trade agreements (Young); addressing greenhouse gas emissions from aviation (Birchfield); and the Maritime Labor Convention (Kissack) – illustrate the argument by representing the three major forms of regulatory co-operation. In addition, each contribution captures within-case variation – among partners (Young) or over time (Birchfield, Kissack) – which permits analysis of the impact of relative power on EU influence.

The two more conceptual contributions by Newman and Posner and by Damro develop the central theme. Newman and Posner present a framework that draws on similar building blocks to explain the EU's external policy strategies, such as creating mutual recognition regimes or establishing first-mover advantage. Rather than take these forms of interaction as exogenous, they seek to explain variation in the form of interaction based on the global regulatory context. In part informed by the contributions to the collection, Damro presents a 'conceptual stock-taking exercise' that attempts to clarify important aspects of the market power Europe (MPE) framework and reflects upon ways in which the conceptualization may offer empirical and analytical contributions that improve our understanding of the EU as a global regulator and, more generally, as a power.

This contribution begins by establishing how pervasive the perception of the EU as an influential regulator beyond its borders is and how this view informs depictions of the EU as a global actor. It then discusses the existing literature on the EU as a global regulator, highlighting the variation in how influence is understood and the fragmentation of the literature. In doing so, it makes the case for treating influence as an ordinal variable. Drawing on the existing

THE EUROPEAN UNION AS A GLOBAL REGULATOR?

regulatory co-operation literature, the contribution develops the argument that the utility of different regulatory power resources varies across forms of regulatory interaction: competition and forms of co-operation. It then illustrates the argument while introducing the empirical contributions. It concludes by drawing out the implications for the analysis of the EU as a global regulator and, in doing so, introducing the rest of the collection.

REGULATION AND THE EU AS A GLOBAL ACTOR

There is a broad consensus that the EU is a regulatory 'great power' (Drezner 2007: 36; Sapir 2007: 12; Scott 2014: 87–8; Vogel 2012: 16; see also Lavanex 2014: 885). Bradford (2012: 5) claims that the EU is 'the predominant regulator of global commerce' (see also Jacoby and Meunier [2010: 306]; Posner [2009: 692]). In the late 2000s the Commission (2007: 5) noted that the EU was 'emerging as a global rule-maker'. The impression of the EU's regulatory influence is echoed in the press, with, for example, The *New York Times* (Lipton and Hakim 2013: A1) calling the EU a 'regulatory superpower' (see also Mitchener [2002]). That the EU's regulations have effects beyond the borders of the single market is, therefore, not in doubt.

This external impact of its regulations is central to depictions of the EU as an international actor (see also Müller *et al.* [2014: 1103]). It is a crucial component of the EU's international 'presence' (Bretherton and Vogler 2006: 27). Cooper (2012) contends that:

> the main output of the Brussels machine are rules that govern trade and that set standards for consumer protection, for the environment, for competition, etc. . . . If the power to make rules is power, then Brussels, in a modest way, is also a power.

In addition, the EU's ability to shape international agreements to reflect its regulations is often equated with 'goal attainment' in the literature assessing the EU's 'performance' in international negotiations (Dee 2013: 49–50; Jørgensen *et al.* 2011: 599). The EU's regulatory impact, therefore, is a crucial component of why it matters in international relations.

For others, the EU's efforts to promote its regulatory choices beyond its borders reveal what type of international actor it is. The EU's coercive promotion of its regulations has led some to label it a 'normative hegemon' (Laïdi 2007: 2–3) and even an 'empire' (Zielonka 2008). Alternatively, the EU's championing of multilateral environmental agreements and promotion of core labour standards is often cited as evidence of the EU being a normative power (Kelemen 2010: 338; Orbie 2011: 160). Damro (2012: 682; 2015), by contrast, contends that the EU 'may be best understood as a market power Europe that exercises its power through the externalization of economic and social market-related policies and regulatory measures'. There is, therefore, despite important differences of emphasis, considerable agreement that the

3

THE EUROPEAN UNION AS A GLOBAL REGULATOR?

EU's rules have significant influence beyond its borders and that this influence shapes understandings of the EU as a global actor.

LIMITATIONS OF THE LITERATURE: OPERATIONALIZATION AND FRAGMENTATION

While there is no denying that the EU's rules matter well beyond its borders, the existing literature has two reinforcing shortcomings that blur the significance of this observation. First, different authors understand regulatory influence in different ways; that is, they effectively, if implicitly, operationalize the dependent variable differently. Second, while the literature on regulatory co-operation has recently begun to examine explicitly variation in EU influence and to consider the importance of the relevant international constellation of power and preferences, it is highly fragmented (see also Müller and Falkner [2014: 1]), advancing explanations with respect to single or closely related cases.

The varied operationalization of influence

Different authors understand what constitutes regulatory influence very differently. For some the focus is the EU's impact on the behaviour of firms. Firms that want to export goods to or provide services in the EU may need to change their practices to secure market access. Having done so, they may opt to comply with EU standards throughout their global operations (see Bradford [2012]; Selin and VanDeveer [2006: 14]; Vogel [2012: 280]; and this is what particularly occupies the press).

For many, if not most, authors regulatory influence is equated with other states changing their rules to align them with those of the EU (Müller and Falkner 2014: 2; Selin and VanDeveer 2006: 14; see also Müller *et al.* 2014: 1103). This is the central focus of the literature on regulatory competition; 'trading up' (Bradford 2012; Selin and VanDeveer 2006; Vogel 1995). It is also the assumption of much of the literature on the EU as a global actor mentioned above. In addition, much of the literature on international regulatory co-operation is also concerned with the question of which state's regulation is adopted as the common one when harmonization occurs (Büthe and Mattli 2011: 9; Dobbin *et al.* 2007: 450; Koenig-Archibugi 2010: 408; Krasner 1991; Simmons 2001). Thus, getting other states to align their rules with its own – 'exporting' its rules – is arguably the 'gold standard' of European regulatory influence.

Other authors also focus on state behaviour, but identify influence in the EU getting the other party to make adjustments to its rules, but not adopt EU rules. In the literature this takes two principal forms. One is the promotion of international standards of which the EU approves (Müller *et al.* 2014: 1109; Young 2015). The other form involves prompting changes that reduce the adverse effects of foreign rules on EU firms, such as by getting states to accept EU

THE EUROPEAN UNION AS A GLOBAL REGULATOR?

rules as equivalent in effect to their own (Bach and Newman 2007: 839; Newman and Posner 2015; Posner 2009: 674–6, 687; Young 2015). In both forms, the EU influences others' rules, but does not export its own.

Other scholars have identified the EU's influence in shaping multilateral agreements. The EU is described as 'exporting' (Kelemen 2010: 341; Newman and Posner 2015) or 'up-loading' (Smith 2010: 937) its rules. Some have found evidence of the EU successfully uploading its regulations into international standard-setting bodies, such as the International Labour Organization (ILO) (Kissack 2011: 657; Tortell *et al.* 2009: 125), the United Nations Economic Commission for Europe (Porter 2011: 80), and the Basel Committee (Quaglia 2014a). Even when the EU uploads its regulations into international standards, other states do not necessarily incorporate those standards into their national rules (Kissack 2011: 658; Quaglia 2014a: 328). Thus, shaping international standards does not necessarily translate into changes in state behaviour.

Other authors highlight the EU's impact on specific steps that lead to an international agreement, such as setting the agenda (Birchfield 2015; Kelemen 2010: 342–4; Newman and Posner 2015; Oberthür and Roche Kelly 2008: 36) or getting other actors to change their positions (Kelemen 2010: 344; Kissack 2015). Yet others (e.g., van Schaik 2013: 111) identify EU influence in its ability to block the adoption of rival standards. The existing literature, therefore, defines the EU's regulatory influence in a variety of ways; it is effectively operationalized differently.

The tendency in the literature is to treat these different operationalizations of influence discreetly and each in a binary fashion. The EU demonstrates the particular manifestation of influence or (usually implicitly) does not, and other understandings are not explicitly considered. Arguably it is more appropriate to treat the different operationalizations as different values of influence that differ considerably in terms of how difficult they are to realize and how significant they are, even leaving aside the magnitude of the change. It is easier to affect the behaviour of firms than the policies of states, and changing a regulation will affect all of the firms in that state. It is easier to get states to adopt international standards rather than European rules because they are more widely accepted and tend to be less demanding (Müller *et al.* 2014: 1109). It is easier to block a rival rule than have one's own adopted as an international standard. How hard it is to block or promote a standard will, all else being equal, depend on the relevant decision rule. It is easier to influence an agreement than to get others to implement and enforce it. In addition, some forms of influence may be prior to others. For instance, agenda-setting and/or shaping the preferences of others may enable the EU to influence an international agreement, which in turn is prior to getting states to change their policies as a result of implementing it. Failure to acknowledge such differences about what constitutes influence has muddied the analytical waters.

Treating the different manifestations of impact as different values of influence converts influence from a fragmented, binary variable to a single, ordinal one,

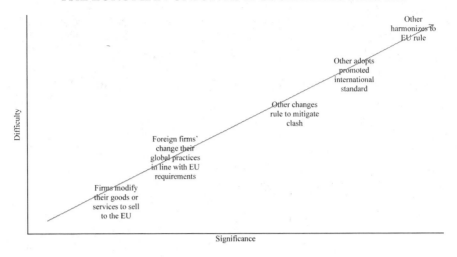

Figure 1 The variable influence of firm behaviour and state policy change

which facilitates comparison among cases. This is the approach adopted in this collection. As the preceding discussion of regulatory influence suggests, it is relatively easy to construct a hierarchy of influence among and within firm behaviour and state policy changes and among outcomes of negotiations, but it is much harder to compare across them. Consequently, I have presented two stylized figures to capture variation in regulatory influence in terms of difficulty and significance: one for firm behaviour and state policy (see Figure 1) and one for multilateral negotiations (see Figure 2). With respect to firms and states, the significance and difficulty of change coincide. In multilateral settings, however, there is not necessarily such co-variation. For instance, *ceteris paribus*,

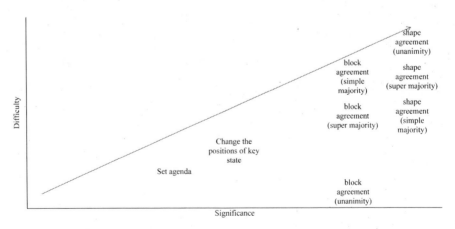

Figure 2 Variable influence in multilateral agreement and international standard setting

THE EUROPEAN UNION AS A GLOBAL REGULATOR?

blocking an agreement is equally significant whether the EU can do so unilaterally or requires the support of numerous others. To be clear, I am not to trying to construct and defend a hierarchy of regulatory influence. Rather, I am making the case that different forms of influence are easier to realize than others and some are more significant than others. The intent is to draw attention to this variability and to provoke exploration and debate.

Belated and fragmented attention to variance in influence

A common point of departure in any new field of study is establishing that the subject is worthy of study. This leads to an understandable tendency to focus on and enumerate instances of the EU's regulatory impact (e.g., Bradford 2012: 30; Damro 2012: 694; Kelemen and Vogel 2010: 428; Vogel 2012: 90; 170). No author claims that the EU influences all firms' behaviour or all states' regulations all of the time. Many authors acknowledge explicitly that it does not, but those instances have only recently been included explicitly in analyses. Consequently, the existing literature is dominated by examples of the EU's influence (however understood). When inferences are drawn from this skewed set of cases, the extent of the EU's influence is exaggerated.

An emphasis on examples of the EU's regulatory influence also has the pernicious effect of inhibiting explanations of the extent and limits of that influence. Establishing how the EU causes others to change their ways requires analysis of examples of both success and failure so as to be able to identify those factors that correlate with the different outcome. Some of the recent literature on regulatory co-operation has begun to do just that (Groen *et al.* 2012; Newman and 2015; Oberthür and Rabitz 2014; Posner 2009; Qualia 2014a). It is on this literature that this contribution draws in the next section.

Much of this literature, however, has focused on individual cases or on variation within a particular issue area (see also Müller and Falkner [2014: 1]).[1] Such a focus on closely related cases has methodological merit because it facilitates isolating the significance of particular variables by keeping others constant. The same approach is adopted in the empirical contributions in this collection. The disadvantage of this tight focus, however, is that it obscures the relevance of broader factors. In particular, it masks how the form of regulatory interaction refracts the EU's regulatory power resources.

REGULATORY INTERACTION AND THE IMPERFECT FUNGIBILITY OF REGULATORY POWER RESOURCES

The global regulation literature identifies two broad forms of regulatory interaction: policy diffusion, in which convergence occurs through one state aligning its policies with another's; and regulatory co-operation, in which alignment comes about through a process of negotiation.[2] Within each of these broad

THE EUROPEAN UNION AS A GLOBAL REGULATOR?

categories are several different forms of interaction (see Table 1). Because of its issue-specific focus, the literature on the EU's regulatory influence overlooks the differences among these forms of interaction. This is problematic because, as the global regulation literature suggests, different regulatory power resources matter more in each.

Although policy diffusion can occur as the result of several different processes (Dobbin *et al.* 2007: 452; Koenig-Archibugi 2010; Lazer 2006: 456), the form of regulatory diffusion that gets by far the most attention in the EU-as-a-global-regulator literature is regulatory competition. The emphasis in the EU literature is primarily on the 'race to the top'/'trading-up' (Vogel [1995]; see also Bradford [2012: 30]; Selin and VanDeveer [2006: 14]). The logic is that foreign firms, having adapted their product or practices in order to gain access to the EU's valuable market, may lobby successfully their home governments to adopt comparable regulations in order to offset the costs of complying with competing requirements and/or to gain advantage over domestically oriented competitors (Bradford 2012: 5; Vogel 1995). Thus, the size (value) of the EU's market, the stringency of its rules and (implicitly) its capacity to enforce them are the key factors affecting the EU's influence through regulatory competition. Although Vogel (1995) put considerable emphasis on the factors that condition whether trading-up occurs, there have been few explicit studies of failures of trading-up (Princen 2004; Young 2003). The resulting tendency to focus on successful cases has also fostered the impression that the EU is particularly influential and the assumption that its regulatory power resources translate relatively smoothly into influence (e.g., Bradford 2012).

The existing literature on the EU's experience of regulatory co-operation, while also tending to accentuate the positive, is much more alive to the limits of EU influence than the literature dealing with regulatory competition. Regulatory co-operation occurs through either power-based bargaining between states outside institutional frameworks or rule-mediated negotiations within international organizations (Büthe and Mattli 2011: 19; Simmons 2001: 598–9; see also Newman and Posner 2015). The literature on regulatory co-operation suggests that different power resources have different utilities in these different types of interaction. The tendency of the regulatory co-operation

Table 1 Forms of regulatory interaction

Diffusion	Co-operation
Competition	Power-based bargaining
[Coercion or inducement through conditionality]	with the prospect of exclusion
[Emulation]	without the prospect of exclusion
[Learning]	Rule-mediated negotiation

THE EUROPEAN UNION AS A GLOBAL REGULATOR?

literature to focus on individual or closely related cases, however, has masked the implications of this insight.

The regulatory co-operation literature has focused on the same regulatory power resources as the regulatory competition literature: market size; rule stringency; and regulatory capacity. Because regulatory co-operation implies strategic interaction and because the EU is an international organization as well as an international actor, there is also an issue about the EU's ability to pursue a common position; to be internally cohesive (Conceição-Heldt and Meunier 2014: 969; Van Schaik 2013: 176). The existence of an EU rule, however, significantly eases the problem of cohesiveness (Quaglia 2014b; Young 2002). Regulatory co-operation authors have also been much more explicit in considering how the EU's power and preferences relate to those of other key actors.

The critical starting assumption in the literature on regulatory co-operation is that each party would prefer its own standard to be adopted as the common one, as this brings benefits without the costs of adjustment (Büthe and Mattli 2011: 12; Drezner 2007: 32). Certainly where the EU has existing rules, which is usually the case, the EU is assumed to want regulatory co-operation to occur on its own terms (Damro 2012: 686; Kelemen 2010: 341; Smith 2010: 937).

When regulatory co-operation takes place outside formal institutions, the form of co-operation is determined by bargaining power, not least because of the distributional implications of the choice of standard (Drezner 2007: 5; Krasner 1991: 336). Bargaining power reflects which party has the better alternative to negotiated agreement (BATNA), which in turn reflects the distribution of costs and benefits stemming from their interdependence (Keohane and Nye 2001: 9; Putnam 1988: 442). The distribution of costs and benefits associated with interdependence are, in turn, profoundly affected by whether the party with the more stringent standard can exclude goods or services that do not comply with that standard from its market (Lazer 2006: 460; Young and Wallace 2000: 24–5). Where exclusion is possible, the party with the more stringent rules has the superior BATNA, as foreign products or service providers are excluded from its market and its firms are protected from competition. When exclusion is not possible, the party with the more stringent regulations tends to have a worse BATNA than its negotiating partner(s). Its firms arguably face higher productions costs, and so are less competitive, and foreign products are not normally excluded from its market. Bargaining power, therefore, is fundamentally different in the two scenarios.

Given sufficient enforcement capacity, exclusion is essentially automatic with respect to stringent product standards. Although the single market's has generally had a liberalizing effect on services (Young and Peterson 2014: 141– 2), there are a few areas in which the EU's rules apply explicitly to service providers based outside the EU. The most prominent examples of such 'territorial extension' (Scott 2014) are in financial services (Dür 2011; Posner 2009); data protection (Newman 2008: Princen 2004). The larger the excluding party's market, the greater the incentive to secure access to the market (Bach and Newman

9

2007: 827; Drezner 2007: 35, 51) and thus to reach accommodation. Given the EU's large market, its generally stringent regulations and its considerable regulatory capacity, the EU's negotiating leverage is formidable in power-based bargaining when exclusion is possible. As in international relations more generally, what matters for influence is relative power (see also Newman and Posner [2015]).

In addition, there is a question as to how much of an adjustment cost foreign firms are willing to incur in order to secure the benefit of greater market access. It is possible that if the EU's regulations are too stringent, the costs of adjustment would outweigh the benefits of co-operation (Drezner 2007: 46–7). Thus, stringent rules are a source of negotiating leverage, but only up to some tipping point. This suggests that relative preferences, reflecting the stringency of existing standards, matter even when exclusion is possible (Young 2015).

The EU's regulatory power resources are much less potent when exclusion is not possible. The most prominent examples of such negotiations are those concerning efforts to address climate change. In this context the EU's market size matters only to the extent that it is part of the problem and its participation is crucial to a solution (McCormick 2007: 158; Oberthür 2011: 677–8). Consequently, the EU has used its regulatory capacity and stringent rules for demonstration effect and to lend its positions legitimacy, rather than for bargaining leverage (Kelemen 2010: 337; Oberthür and Roche Kelly: 2008: 36).

The literature on bargaining without exclusion also highlights the importance of the EU's preferences relative to those of other actors and to the *status quo*. The EU is less likely to affect the outcome if it is pushing for change (is 'reformist') and is a preference outlier (Groen *et al.* 2012: 185). Where the EU's position is 'conservative', preferring the *status quo*, the EU's economic importance means others have an incentive to accommodate it in order to secure its participation and enhance the significance of the agreement (Oberthür and Rabitz 2013: 2). In addition, the EU's cohesiveness may be undermined if its negotiating position goes beyond what has already been adopted internally (Groen *et al.* 2012: 184). Thus, for a variety of reasons, when exclusion is not possible, stringent standards and a large market do not lend negotiating leverage to nearly the same extent as they do when exclusion is possible.

The implications for the utility of regulatory power resources are similar within formal, state-centric international standard setting bodies, where decision-making is rule-mediated. The critical difference is that, although the norm in international standard-setting bodies is to seek consensus, some can take decisions by voting. Because the EU's member states are individually members of international standard-setting bodies, voting does give the EU greater weight than other actors. That greater weight, however, depends on the EU having a cohesive position (Quaglia 2014a: 328; Kissack 2015). When voting is possible, despite its vote advantage, the EU is rarely able on its own to block standards that it does not like, although it need not implement them. The EU's market size, therefore, matters only in the sense that a standard implemented by the world's largest market is more valuable than one that it

THE EUROPEAN UNION AS A GLOBAL REGULATOR?

ignores (Quaglia 2014a: 328). In some circumstances, however, the EU may be able to exploit its economic weight to influence the preferences of states within the standard setting body, as occurred with the Maritime Labour Convention (Kissack 2015).

Regulatory capacity, in terms of being able to gather and generate information and aggregate preferences, is particularly important in shaping negotiations in international standard-setting bodies (Büthe and Mattli 2011: 12-13; King and Narlikar 2003). Stringent rules, however, increase the likelihood that the EU will be a preference outlier and thus reduce the likelihood that agreed international standards will reflect its own (Young 2014). Thus, *ceteris paribus*, the EU's regulatory power resources are less significant with respect to rule-mediated standard setting than they are in power-based bargaining when exclusion is possible, but somewhat more so than in power-based bargaining when it is not.

The literature on regulatory co-operation, particularly that on bargaining without the possibility of exclusion and rule-mediated negotiations, also challenges the assumption that the EU always seeks to export its rules. Because regulatory co-operation involves strategic interaction, the EU at times advances progressive positions that are less extreme than its own rules in an effort to increase the likelihood of agreement (Goen *et al.* 2012: 185; Mair 2008: 21-2; Van Schaik 2013: 106-8). Such moderation has been less observed in power-based bargaining when exclusion is possible. Nonetheless, it is reasonable to expect the EU to shy away from insisting on harmonization on its terms, even when exclusion is possible, if the adjustment costs are sufficiently high that doing so might scupper an agreement that brings other benefits. This is certainly what seems to be happening in the EU's 'new generation' preferential trade agreements (Young 2015). Thus, how the EU's preferences relate to those of others can affect not just its ability to realize its objectives, but also how ambitious those objectives are (Dee 2013: 225; Groen *et al.* 2012); whether it even tries to export its rules.

This discussion of the literature on the EU's engagement in regulatory co-operation prompts three takeaways for the collection. First, the utility of the EU's regulatory power resources varies systematically depending on the form of regulatory interaction, including among forms of co-operation: whether it is power-based bargaining with or without the possibility of exclusion or rule-mediated negotiation. This insight has been obscured by the tendency of the literature to focus on individual or closely related cases that fall within the same form of regulatory co-operation. Second, how cohesive the positions of the EU's member states are is a live consideration when dealing with regulatory co-operation, in a way that it is not when dealing with policy diffusion. Third, explanations of the EU's influence need to look beyond the EU's resources to consider how its preferences and power relate to those of other key actors. In short, context – the form of regulatory co-operation, relative power and relative preferences – matter. The significance of these insights is illustrated by the empirical contributions to this collection.

THE EUROPEAN UNION AS A GLOBAL REGULATOR?

INTRODUCING THE EMPIRICAL CONTRIBUTIONS: ILLUSTRATING THE ARGUMENT

The central argument of this contribution is that the utility of the EU's regulatory power resources varies systematically across the forms of regulatory interaction, including among forms of co-operation, the focus of this collection. The form of regulatory co-operation, therefore, is a critical variable that affects how the EU's power resources translate into influence. Each of the three empirical contributions falls within one of the three forms of regulatory co-operation at any given time. The new generation preferential trade agreements (Young) represent bargaining with exclusion. The aviation emissions case (Birchfield) begins as bargaining without exclusion, but with the EU's decision to incorporate flights outside the EU within the Emissions Trading System (ETS), it becomes bargaining with the prospect of exclusion. The Maritime Labour Convention (Kissack) reflects rule-mediated negotiation. Together, therefore, the three cases permit exploration of the impact of the form of regulatory co-operation on influence.

The subcases within each of the three empirical contributions capture variation in the EU's relative regulatory resources; that is, there is within-case variation in the relative power of the EU's partners. The EU has negotiated preferential trade agreements with countries that differ both in their economic size and their regulatory capacity. In the aviation emissions case the EU's effective power resources increased as a result of creating the possibility of exclusion. In the maritime labour case the EU's effective power resources increased once it began advancing common positions from 2003. Thus, in addition to capturing within-case variation, the empirical contributions also represent different ways in which the EU's relative regulatory resources can vary.

As the motivating question here is what explains the EU's ability to influence regulations beyond its borders, the presumption is that the EU is seeking change away from the *status quo* towards its preferences; that is, it has adopted a 'progressive' position. As the literature notes, the degree to which the EU is progressive can vary. It can be ambitious or more moderate. Here an ambitious objective is defined as the EU seeking to secure its ideal outcome, such as adoption of its regulatory solution. In such cases the EU is often a preference outlier. A more moderate position involves the EU adopting a position closer to the *status quo* than its ideal outcome. In such instances, its position is more likely to be shared or supported by other actors. The assessment of how progressive the EU's preferences are thus captures how its preferences relate both to the *status quo* and to those of other actors. The cases capture different levels of ambition, with it being least ambitious in the Maritime Labour Convention and most ambitious with respect to aviation emissions.

The subcases in the empirical contributions also capture substantial variation in the degree of EU influence. The most demanding form of influence is found with respect to the EU's preferential trade agreements, where some parties agreed to change some of their rules to conform to international standards (Young 2015). In the Maritime Labour Convention, once the EU's member states began presenting common positions, they collectively shaped aspects of the agreement, although even then they were not universally successful and many of the important issues had been settled before they began co-ordinating (Kissack 2015). In addition, that the EU's member states could enforce the agreed standards on all ships entering their ports caused flag-states and ship-owners to moderate their opposition so as to be able to shape the rules. In the aviation emissions case (Birchfield 2015) after the EU decided to include aviation in the ETS other key players agreed to put the issue seriously on the agenda of the International Civil Aviation Organization (ICAO). Prior to the inclusion of aviation in the ETS and prior to EU co-ordination on maritime labour standards, the EU effectively had no influence. The EU's degree of influence across the cases therefore ranges from none through agenda-setting and influencing the positions of negotiating partners to securing commitments to adopt international standards (convergence).

The findings from the three empirical chapters (summarized in Table 2) testify to the importance of the variation in the EU's power resources across different forms of regulatory co-operation. The EU's influence is greatest with respect to power-based bargaining with exclusion; prompting some policy convergence in preferential trading agreements. It is particularly telling that the decision to include aviation in the ETS, which transformed the power-based bargaining from without exclusion to with the possibility of exclusion, coincided with a sharp increase in the EU's influence, from none discernable to getting the issue on ICAO's agenda. As predicted, the EU's influence within the rule-mediated negotiation on the Maritime Labour Convention presents an intermediate case with the EU getting its way on some provisions, but not others. This analysis strongly suggests that scholars should take the form of regulatory co-operation seriously when analysing the EU's regulatory influence.

In addition, the variation in the EU's influence within the cases is consistent with explanations advanced in the existing literature. The EU had greater influence in PTAs with smaller partners with lower regulatory capacities than with larger partners. The EU's influence in the Maritime Labour Convention increased once its internal cohesiveness increased as the member states began co-ordinating their positions. The inclusion of aviation emissions on the ICAO agenda came in response to the decision to include aviation in the ETS. The impact of how the EU's preferences relate to those of others, however, could not be assessed on the basis of the cases. There is no within-case variation on the preferences of other actors in the cases of aviation and maritime labour. In the PTA cases the EU's ambition co-varied with the power of partners; seeking more ambitious outcomes with the least powerful than the most powerful. Significantly, however, while observed variance is in line with expectations about the importance of relative power, the magnitude of influence across the board is considerably less that suggested by the common view of the

THE EUROPEAN UNION AS A GLOBAL REGULATOR?

EU as a global regulator. This observation is consistent with the form of regulatory interaction being a critical variable.

CONCLUSIONS

There are three overarching conclusions to draw from the contributions to this volume. The first, which is to the fore in this contribution, is that the utility of the EU's regulatory power resources is context specific. The second is that, at least as previously conceived, the debates about what kind of power the EU is have been unproductive. The third, which builds on the second, is that the EU's engagement in the world does not need to be studied through bespoke theories. Rather, it is better explained through more general theories of international political economy. These arguments are advanced explicitly in the contributions by Newman and Posner and Damro, motivated this contribution and are illustrated by the analyses in the empirical cases of preferential trade agreements (Young); the Maritime Labour Convention (Kissack) and efforts to address aviation emissions (Birchfield).

The need to attend to context is a central claim of this contribution and of that by Newman and Posner. This contribution has argued that the EU's influence varies systematically across the different forms of regulatory co-operation. The utility of the EU's regulatory power resources is greatest when co-operation takes place through bargaining and foreign products or firms can be excluded from the EU's market. It is least when bargaining occurs, but exclusion is not possible. Rule-mediated negotiation represents an intermediate case. The empirical chapters in this collection illustrate this argument. The EU's influence is greatest – prompting rule change – in preferential trade agreements, which have the form of power-based bargain with the prospect of exclusion. The EU's efforts to have greenhouse gas emissions from aviation addressed at the global level went nowhere when bargaining occurred without the prospect of exclusion, but the decision to include aviation in the EU's Emissions Trading System, thereby providing for exclusion, led to the issue being placed on the agenda of the International Civil Aviation Organization. In the negotiations over the Maritime Labour Convention within the International Labour Organization, the EU had some influence on the agreement once it started co-ordinating its position, but even then only prevailed on some issues. Thus, the form of regulatory co-operation is a critical variable that refracts how the EU's regulatory power resources translate into influence.

Newman and Posner highlight that the EU's strategies for realizing its regulatory objectives reflect the interaction of its regulatory capacity relative to that of other key regulatory powers and of the institutional density at the global level. These strategic choices influence the forms of regulatory interaction discussed in this contribution. This contribution too points to the importance of relative regulatory power in explaining EU influence, albeit with a more expansive conceptualization that goes beyond Newman and Posner's regulatory capacity. The empirical cases provide support for the importance of relative regulatory power.

THE EUROPEAN UNION AS A GLOBAL REGULATOR?

In the case of PTAs, the EU's influence was greatest where its relative power was greatest – Central America – and seems certain to be most limited with respect to its peer – the United States. The EU's influence on the Maritime Labour Convention increased markedly once the member states began co-ordinating their positions. A key takeaway from this volume therefore is that how the EU pursues its regulatory objectives and whether it is able to realize them is highly contingent on factors beyond the EU; context matters. A focus on just the EU's power attributes therefore is inadequate for analysing the EU as a global regulator.

Such a focus on only EU attributes, however, has been a common feature of the literatures on the EU-as-a-global actor and as-a-global regulator (see also Newman and Posner [2015] and Damro [2015]). This shortcoming has been compounded by the tendency of the rival claims to talk past each other. Both Damro and Newman and Posner observe that the civilian power Europe accounts emphasize coercion and costs and benefits, while normative power Europe accounts emphasize ideas and persuasion as sources of power. Moreover, contending depictions of Europe as a power tend to align coercion with material interests and persuasion with ideational or normative motivations as competing sources of power (see also Damro [2015]). The empirical contributions to this collection, however, highlight how such distinctions are unhelpful. With respect to both the Maritime Labour Convention and aviation emissions, the EU promoted norms – human rights and sustainable development – in multilateral fora in part through its ability to unilaterally impose costs on its negotiating partners (Birchfield 2015; Kissack 2015). The PTA case is somewhat more ambiguous as here the EU promoted human rights and environmental norms through non-binding provisions, in stark contrast to the United States, but the promotion of these norms was inextricably linked to efforts to secure enhanced market access (Young 2015). The second takeaway from this collection therefore is the need for a more constructive debate among the competing conceptualizations of the EU as a power.

The contributions by Newman and Posner and Damro suggest different ways in which this conversation might be taken forward. Newman and Posner contend that both normative and civilian/market conceptualizations can be subsumed by an emphasis on regulatory capacity, which captures both the ideas motivating policy and the costs of not complying with it. Damro explores the utility of employing market power Europe as an explicit conceptual framework to capture the impact of those (and other) factors in a manner that takes forward the debate.

The third conclusion from this collection is that a crucial contribution to advancing such a constructive debate is grounding the analysis of the EU as a global regulator in general theories of international political economy. This case is advanced explicitly by Newman and Posner and Damro and implicitly (until now) by this contribution. The empirical contributions illustrate the suitability of this approach. Critically, using general theories to explain EU influence not only helps us to understand the EU better, but means that insights

16

THE EUROPEAN UNION AS A GLOBAL REGULATOR?

gained from the study of the EU can apply to other international actors (see also Newman and Posner [2015] and Damro [2015]). There is thus every reason to expect the influence of the US, the other great regulator, to vary across forms of regulatory co-operation. Likewise other actors' strategies for pursuing regulatory objectives will vary depending on their relative regulatory capacity and the degree of international institutionalization. Given its focus on the EU, this collection does not make this case, but its approach, rooted in general theories of comparative and international political economy, makes this a plausible further line of enquiry.

Biographical note: Alasdair Young is professor of international affairs and Jean Monnet Chair in the Sam Nunn School of International Affairs, Georgia Institute of Technology. He is also chair of the European Union Studies Association (2015–17).

ACKNOWLEDGEMENTS

This contribution is part of a wider project that has been funded with support from the European Commission (Jean Monnet Chair 2012-3121). It reflects the views only of the author, and the Commission cannot be held responsible for any use which may be made of the information contained herein. Earlier versions of this contribution were presented at the 'Regulatory Power Europe? Assessing the EU's Efforts to Shape Global Rules' Jean Monnet Chair Workshop, Georgia Institute of Technology, 18–19 April 2014, and the 14th Biennial Conference of the European Union Studies Association, Boston, 5–7 March 2015. I am grateful Vicki Birchfield, Chad Damro, Robert Kissack, Sandra Lavenex, Abraham Newman, Elliot Posner, Jamal Shahin, Mike Smith, Kazuto Suzuki and two anonymous referees for their comments. I assert sole ownership of all errors and omissions.

NOTES

1 There are two partial exceptions. Both Drezner (2007) and Müller and Falkner (2014) consider a wide range of policies that fall within different forms of regulatory interaction. In neither case, however, is the focus explicitly on influence. Drezner analyses the likelihood of regulatory co-ordination, with an emphasis on the degree of great power agreement. In addition, he does not explicitly consider the relevance of different contexts on the interaction among the great powers. Müller and Falkner's (2014: 6) main concern is the form of interaction and whether the EU has tended to export, import or protect its rules. There is a very limited focus on explaining the observed variation (Falkner and Müller 2014: 223–4).

2 Simmons (2001: 598–9) distinguishes between 'market' and 'political' mechanisms. Bütte and Mattli (2011: 19) distinguish between 'market' and 'non-market'

THE EUROPEAN UNION AS A GLOBAL REGULATOR?

mechanisms. Koenig-Archibugi (2010: 408), Lazer (2006: 456) and Holzinger *et al.* (2008: 556) draw tri-partite distinctions, but these include one co-operative mechanism and two policy diffusion mechanisms. Müller and Falkner (2014: 8) identify four mechanisms: 'bargaining' (co-operation) and three forms of diffusion.

REFERENCES

Bach, D. and Newman, A.L. (2007) 'The European regulatory state and global public policy: micro-institutions, macro-influence', *Journal of European Public Policy* 14(6): 827–46.

Birchfield, V. (2015) 'Coercion with kid gloves: the European Union's role in shaping a global regulatory framework for aviation emissions', *Journal of European Public Policy*, doi: 10.1080/13501763.2015.1046904.

Bradford, A. (2012) 'The Brussels effect', *Northwestern University Law Review* 107(1): 1–68.

Bretherton, C. and Vogler, J. (2006) *The European Union as a Global Actor*, 2nd edn, London: Routledge.

Büthe, T. and Mattli, W. (2011) *The New Global Rulers: The Privatization of Regulation in the WorldEconomy*, Princeton, NJ: Princeton University Press.

Commission (2007) 'The external dimension of the Single Market review', *SEC(2007) 1519*, 20 November, Brussels: Commission of the European Communities.

Conceição-Heldt, E. da and Meunier, S. (2014) 'Speaking with a single voice: internal cohesiveness and external effectiveness of the EU in global governance', *Journal of European Public Policy* 21(7): 961–79.

Cooper, R. (2012) 'Hubris and false hopes', *Policy Review*, 172, 30 March.

Damro, C. (2012) 'Market power Europe', *Journal of European Public Policy* 19(5): 682–99.

Damro, C. (2015) Market power Europe: exploring a dynamic conceptual framework', *Journal of European Public Policy*, doi: 10.1080/13501763.2015.1046903.

Dee, M. (2013) 'Challenging expectations: a study of European Union performance in multilateral negotiations', Ph.D. thesis, University of Glasgow.

Dobbin, F., Simmons, B. and Garret, G. (2007) 'The global diffusion of public policies: social construction, coercion, competition or learning?', *Annual Review of Sociology* 33: 449–72.

Drezner, D.W. (2007) *All Politics is Global: Explaining International Regulatory Regimes*, Princeton, NJ: Princeton University Press.

Dür, A. (2011) 'Fortress Europe or open door Europe? The external impact of the EU's single market in financial services', *Journal of European Public Policy* 18(5): 619–35.

Groen, L., Niemann, A. and Oberthür, S. (2012) 'The EU as a global leader? The Copenhagen and Cancun UN climate change negotiations', *Journal of Contemporary European Research* 8(2): 173–91.

Holzinger, K., Knill, C. and Sommerer, T. (2008) 'Environmental policy convergence: the impact of international harmonization, transnational communication and regulatory competition', *International Organization* 62(fall): 553–87.

Jacoby, W. and Meunier, S. (2010) 'Europe and the management of globalization', *Journal of European Public Policy* 17(3): 299–317.

Jørgensen, K.E., Oberthür, S. and Shahin, J. (2011) 'Introduction: assessing the EU's performance in international institutions – conceptual framework and core findings', *Journal of European Integration* 33(6): 599–620.

Kelemen, D. (2010) 'Globalizing European Union environmental policy', *Journal of European Public Policy* 17(3): 335–49.

THE EUROPEAN UNION AS A GLOBAL REGULATOR?

Kelemen, R.D. and Vogel, D. (2010) 'Trading places: the role of the United States and the European Union in international environmental politics', *Comparative Political Studies* 43(4): 427–56.

Keohane, R.O. and Nye, J.S. (2001) *Power and Interdependence*, 3rd edn, New York: Longman.

King, D. and Narlikar, A. (2003) 'The new risk regulators? International organisations and globalisation', *The Political Quarterly* 74(3): 337–48.

Kissack, R. (2011) 'The performance of the European Union in the international labour organization', *Journal of European Integration* 33(6): 651–65.

Kissack, R. (2015) 'Man overboard!' Was EU influence on the Maritime Labour Convention lost at sea?', *Journal of European Public Policy*, doi: 10.1080/13501763.2015.1046899.

Koenig-Archibugi, M. (2010) 'Global regulation', in R. Baldwin, M. Cave and D. Lodge (eds), *The Oxford Handbook of Regulation*, Oxford: Oxford University Press, pp. 406–33.

Krasner, S.D. (1991) 'Global communications and national power: life on the Pareto frontier', *World Politics* 43(3): 336–66.

Laïdi, Z. (2007) *The Unintended Consequences of European Power*, Les Cahiers européene de Sciences Po, ñ 05, Paris: Centre d'études européenes at Sciences Po.

Lavenex, S. (2014) 'The power of functionalist extension: How EU rules travel', *Journal of European Public Policy* 21(6): 885–903.

Lazer, D. (2006) 'Global and domestic governance: modes of interdependence in regulatory policymaking', *European Law Journal* 12(4): 455–68.

Mair, M.L. (2008) 'The regulatory state goes global: EU participation in international food standard-setting by the Codex Alimentarius Commission', Paper presented at the GARNET conference on 'The European Union in International Affairs', Institute for European Studies, Vrije Universiteit, Brussel, 24–26 April.

Lipton, E. and Hakim, D. (2013) 'Lobbying bonanza as firms try to influence European Union,' *New York Times*, 18 October, p. A1.

McCormick, J. (2007) *The European Superpower*, Basingstoke: Palgrave MacMillan.

Mitchener, B. (2002) 'Rules, regulations of global economy are increasingly being set in Brussels,' *Wall Street Journal*, 23 April.

Müller, P. and Falkner, G. (2014) 'The EU as a policy exporter? The conceptual framework', in G. Falkner and P. Müller (eds.), *EU Policies in a Global Perspective: Shaping or Taking International Regimes?* London: Routledge, pp. 1–19.

Müller, P., Kudrna, Z. and Falkner, G. (2014) 'EU–global interactions: policy export, import, promotion and protection', *Journal of European Public Policy* 21(8): 1102–19.

Newman, A.L. (2008) *Protectors of Privacy: Regulating Personal Data in the Global Economy*, Ithaca, NY: Cornell University Press.

Newman, A.L. and Posner, E. (2015) 'Putting the EU in its place: policy strategies and the global regulatory context', *Journal of European Public Policy*, doi: 10.1080/13501763.2015.1046901.

Oberthür S. (2011) 'The European Union's performance in the international climate change regime', *Journal of European Integration* 33(6): 667–82

Oberthür, S. and Rabitz, F. (2014) 'On the EU's performance and leadership in global environmental governance: the case of the Nagoya Protocol', *Journal of European Public Policy* 21(1): 39–57.

Oberthür, S. and Roche Kelly, C. (2008) 'EU leadership in international climate policy: achievements and challenges', *The International Spectator* 43(3): 35–50.

Orbie, J. (2011) 'Promoting labour standards through trade: normative power or regulatory state Europe', in R. G. Whitman (ed.), *Normative Power Europe: Empirical and Theoretical Perspectives*, Basingstoke: PalgraveMacmillan, pp. 160–83.

Porter, T. (2011) 'Transnational policy paradigm change and conflict in the harmonization of vehicle safety and accounting standards', in G. Skogstad (ed.), *Policy Paradigms: Transnationalism and Domestic Politics*, Toronto: University of Toronto Press, pp. 64–90.

Posner, E. (2009) 'Making rules for global finance: transatlantic regulatory co-operation at the turn of the millennium', *International Organization* 63(4): 665–99.

Princen, S. (2004) 'Trading up in the transatlantic relationship', *Journal of Public Policy* 24(1): 127–44.

Putnam, R.D. (1988) 'Diplomacy and domestic politics: the logic of two-level games', *International Organization* 42(3): 427–60.

Quaglia, L. (2014a) 'The sources of European Union influence in international financial regulatory fora', *Journal of European Public Policy* 21(3): 327–45.

Quaglia, L. (2014b) 'The European Union, the USA and international standard setting by regulatory fora in finance', *New Political Economy* 19(3): 427–44.

Sapir, A. (2007) 'Europe and the global economy', in A. Sapir (ed.), *Fragmented Power: Europe and the Global Economy*, Brussels: Bruegel, pp. 1–20.

Scott, J. (2014). 'Extraterritoriality and territorial extension in EU law', *American Journal of Comparative Law* 62(1): 87–125.

Selin, H. and VanDeveer, S.D. (2006) 'Raising global standards: hazardous substances and e-waste management in the European Union', *Environment* 48(10): 6–17.

Simmons, B.A. (2001) 'The international politics of harmonization: the case of capital market regulation', *International Organization* 55(3): 589–620.

Smith, M.P. (2010) 'Single market, global competition: regulating the European economy in a global economy', *Journal of European Public Policy* 17(7): 936–53.

Tortell, L., Delarue, R. and Kenner, J. (2009) 'The EU and the ILO Maritime Labour Convention', in J. Orbie and L. Tortell (eds), *The European Union and the Social Dimension of Globalization: How the EU influences the World*, London: Routlege, pp. 113–30.

van Schaik, L.G. (2013) *EU Effectiveness and Unity in Multilateral Negotiations: More than the Sum of Its Parts?* Basingstoke: Palgrave Macmillan.

Vogel, D. (1995) *Trading Up: Consumer and Environmental Regulation in a Global Economy*, Cambridge, MA: Harvard University Press.

Vogel, D. (2012) *The Politics of Precaution: Regulating Health, Safety, and Environmental Risks in Europe and the United States*, Princeton, NJ: Princeton University Press.

Young, A.R. (2002) *Extending European Cooperation: The European Union and the 'New' International Trade Agenda*, Manchester: Manchester University Press.

Young, A.R. (2003) 'Political transfer and "trading up": transatlantic trade in genetically modified food and US politics', *World Politics* 55(4): 457–84.

Young, A.R. (2014) 'Europe as a global regulator? The limits of EU influence in international food safety standards', *Journal of European Public Policy* 21(6): 904–22.

Young, A.R. (2015) 'Liberalizing trade, not exporting rules: the limits to regulatory coordination in the EU's "new generation:" preferential trade agreements', *Journal of European Public Policy*, doi: 10.1080/13501763.2015.1046900.

Young, A.R. and Peterson, J. (2014) *Parochial Global Europe: 21st Century Trade Politics*, Oxford: Oxford University Press.

Young, A.R. and Wallace (2000) *Regulatory Politics in the Enlarging European Union: Weighing Civic and Producer Interests*, Manchester: Manchester University Press.

Zielonka, J. (2008) 'Europe as a global actor: empire by example?' *International Affair*, 84(3): 471–84.

agreements and increased attention to regulatory barriers to trade since its 2006 'Global Europe' strategy.

There are several reasons to expect the EU to export its regulations through these so-called 'new generation' PTAs. First, the EU is known to use trade policy to promote domestic policy changes unrelated to trade. Second, the European Commission's rhetoric suggests the objective of encouraging others to adopt EU rules. Third, analyses of the EU's earlier PTAs claim that it puts a distinctively heavy emphasis on regulatory harmonization. Fourth, the negotiation of PTAs takes place through power-based bargaining with the possibility of exclusion, which is identified in the introduction (Young 2015) as the form of international regulatory co-operation through which the EU is most likely to be able to export its rules. This contribution, however, demonstrates that the EU has not exported its regulations through 'new generation' PTAs. Moreover, it contends that the EU has not really tried to. It speculates that the EU has not sought to export aggressively its rules through new generation PTAs because of concern that opposition to regulatory change in its partners would jeopardize agreements that would benefit European firms. The EU, therefore, is exporting goods and services, not exporting rules.

To make this argument, this contribution analyses four of the EU's new generation PTAs – those with Canada, Central America, Singapore and South Korea – and its negotiating positions with respect to the United States. It considers a range of regulatory measures: technical barriers to trade; sanitary and phytosanitary measures; domestic regulation of financial services; competition policy; data protection; environmental protection; and labour standards. Across this diverse array of partners and types of regulation, this contribution identifies efforts to mitigate and even narrow regulatory differences, but no evidence of the EU exporting its rules. That said, the EU's regulatory influence does seem to vary in line with the power of its partner. The magnitude of that influence across the board, however, is much less than suggested by the EU-as-a-global-regulator literature.

This contribution begins by setting out why one should expect the EU to export its regulations through bilateral trade diplomacy before introducing the EU's renewed emphasis on addressing regulatory differences through PTAs. It then introduces the dynamics of regulatory co-ordination before surveying the regulatory co-operation provisions in the EU's new generation PTAs. It then considers why the EU has not exported its rules through the new generation PTAs and reflects on the implications for our understanding of the EU as a global regulator.

EXPORTING RULES THROUGH BILATERAL TRADE AGREEMENTS?

A substantial strand of the EU-as-a-global-actor literature is concerned with the extent to which the EU seeks to promote its values and norms through trade policy (see Young and Peterson 2014: 183). Meunier and Nicolaïdis (2006:

THE EUROPEAN UNION AS A GLOBAL REGULATOR?

907) characterize the EU is a 'trade power' that is able to 'export' its laws and standards to other countries by offering improved access to its large and valuable market (see also Garcia [2013: 535]; Müller and Falkner [2014: 11–12]). Then Trade Commissioner Karel De Gucht (2010: 3) described trade policy as one of the key 'vectors' for promoting the EU's values and principles. Comparative analyses find that the EU, unusually, tends to include provisions on the harmonization of product regulations in its PTAs (Piermartini and Budetta 2009: 291; Stoler 2011: 217; World Trade Organization [WTO] 2011: 142). Thus there is a common view that the EU exports its rules through trade policy.

This consensus, however, is heavily influenced by PTAs with countries with particularly close economic and political relations with the EU – countries in its 'neighbourhood' and the African, Caribbean and Pacific (ACP) countries (Piermartini and Budetta 2009: 292–3; WTO 2011: 142, 157–8). This tendency should not, however, be assumed to hold with countries less economically and politically connected to the EU. Moreover, Woolcock (2007: 4), informed by largely the same population of agreements, disagrees with the assessment, contending that the EU has 'not been very aggressive in pushing for harmonization' based on its rules. There is thus an open question about whether the EU has sought to export its regulatory choices through its 'new generation' PTAs.

REGULATORY DIFFERENCES: A NEW TRADE PRIORITY

The issue of the EU's efforts to export its regulations through PTAs came to the fore in the latter half of the 2000s as the result of changes in the EU's trade strategy (for a discussion, see Young and Peterson [2014: 63–4]). One change, first articulated in the Commission's 2006 Global Europe communication, was to put new emphasis on bilateral trade relations with economically significant parties. The 2010 Europe 2020 trade strategy doubled down on this approach. Prior to 2006 the EU had PTAs with three non-neighbourhood and non-ACP countries: Chile; Mexico; and South Africa. In the eight years after 2006, the EU concluded negotiations of five such agreements and had launched seven more. Should these negotiations be successfully concluded, more than two-thirds of EU trade will be covered by PTAs, up from less than a quarter before 2006 (Commission 2013a: 4).

The second change in EU trade policy was to increase the emphasis on regulatory barriers to trade. In its first market access strategy the Commission (1996: 4) identified two trade objectives, one of which was 'to encourage our trading partners to adopt standards and regulatory approaches based on, or compatible with international and European practice'. The Global Europe communication called for 'regulatory convergence wherever possible' (Commission 2006: 9). In a follow-up communication to its 2020 trade strategy, the Commission (2013a: 5) identified 'tackling complex regulatory issues' as a key condition for advancing the EU's trade agenda to promote jobs and growth. As a consequence, regulatory co-operation has moved to the centre of the EU's increasingly ambitious

THE EUROPEAN UNION AS A GLOBAL REGULATOR?

bilateral trade agenda. It is these 'new generation' PTAs that are the focus of this analysis.

FORMS OF CO-ORDINATION

Because the adverse trade effects of domestic regulations are usually side-effects of realizing other policy objectives, they, unlike tariffs, cannot simply be traded away. Regulatory co-operation, therefore, focuses on how to liberalize trade while still achieving the underlying public policy objectives (Organization for Economic Co-operation and Development [OECD] 2013: 15). There is a tendency in the literature on international regulatory co-operation to assume that the means to square this circle is through harmonization – the adoption of a common rule by both parties (Koenig-Archibugi 2010: 416). For the EU to be exporting its rules though PTAs, harmonization must be based on its rule.

Harmonization, however, is only one form of regulatory co-operation. While the spectrum of regulatory co-operation is vast, this contribution considers only concrete efforts to address current trade concerns stemming from differences in national regulations. This emphasis aligns with what Drezner (2007: 11) terms 'regulatory coordination,' which is 'the codified adjustment of national standards in order to recognize or accommodate regulatory frameworks from other countries'.

Drezner draws useful distinctions between co-ordination, convergence and harmonization. Convergence means that the parties' rules become more similar without necessarily becoming the same, which would constitute harmonization. Moreover, the parties can mitigate the adverse trade effects of their rules (co-ordinate) by accepting that the other's rule as it stands is equivalent in effect to its own, establishing equivalence, but implying no convergence. Regulatory co-ordination can also include aligning data and testing requirements and accepting the other party's certification of conformity. While such changes can have important trade effects, the do not affect the regulations themselves, so I (rather unfairly) include such efforts in 'no co-ordination'. For the purposes of analysis, therefore, the regulatory co-operation in the EU's PTAs can have one of four 'values': no co-ordination; equivalence; convergence; or harmonization.

The distinctions between the three forms of regulatory co-ordination, however, are not always clear cut. For instance, Piermartini and Budetta (2009: 270) consider the parties agreeing to a common rule or committing to use international standards to be harmonization. Woolcock (2007: 4), by contrast, equates harmonization with the adoption of EU rules. Using Piermartini and Budetta's (2009: Annex 2) own coding, only one EU PTA in their analysis calls for harmonization using this narrower definition (down from 12), which goes a long way to explaining the vastly different assessments of the EU's emphasis on harmonization mentioned earlier. As international standards tend to differ from EU regulations, I consider agreeing to change national rules to align with existing international standards to be an example of convergence, rather than harmonization (see also Müller *et al.* [2014: 1108–9]).

Just as the distinction between convergence and harmonization can be blurred, so too can be the distinction between convergence and equivalence. In particular, it is not uncommon for a degree of convergence to be necessary before equivalence is accepted (OECD 2013: 55). I consider such cases to be instances of convergence. Pure equivalence occurs only when no changes to existing rules are required. Equivalence thus implies no export of the EU's rules. Only where harmonization occurs on the basis of the EU's rule can the EU be considered to have truly exported its rule. The EU can, however, also be considered to have exercised regulatory influence when the other party undertakes to make its rules more similar to, but not the same as, the EU's (convergence) (see also Müller *et al.* [2014]).

EXPLAINING REGULATORY CO-ORDINATION

As the form of regulatory co-ordination has bearing on whether the EU can be considered to have exported it rules, understanding what shapes the choice of form is pertinent to explaining when the EU is more likely to export its rules. This section explores the politics shaping the choice of form of regulatory co-ordination, as well as its substance. It thus lays the foundations for expectations about when the EU is more likely to export its rules.

An important point of departure is to recognize that regulatory co-ordination is politically and administratively more complicated than traditional trade liberalization. As noted earlier, regulations normally have objectives other than restricting trade that still need to be realized. As a consequence and as I shall elaborate in a moment, regulatory co-ordination may impose adjustment costs on export-oriented firms, the traditional supporters of liberalization, as well as import-competing ones. Their support, therefore, may well be more conditional than in a traditional trade negotiation. In addition, regulations tend to be rooted in domestic regulatory processes. Changes to regulation may require legislatures to change domestic laws or regulators to adopt new rules. These requirements introduce more veto players into the policy process, which makes policy change harder. Further, consumer and environmental groups, at least in developed countries, tend to be much more actively engaged when trade policy touches on regulation (Young and Peterson 2006). While traditional liberalization tends to bring only benefits to consumers, regulatory co-ordination risks also bringing costs in the form of less safe or more environmentally harmful products, although, where domestic protections are considered inadequate, co-ordination may be seen as a way to import stringency (e.g., Sierra Club [2013: 4]). For these reasons, international regulatory co-ordination is very difficult and is thus rare (OECD 2013: 54; 14). Unfortunately, the existing literature on regulatory co-ordination is much better at explaining the form of regulatory co-ordination should it occur than at explaining whether it will occur.

THE EUROPEAN UNION AS A GLOBAL REGULATOR?

Explanations of regulatory harmonization are most developed in the literature. While export-oriented firms on both sides would gain from having to deal with only one rule, each would prefer to avoid incurring the costs of adjusting to that rule (Büthe and Mattli 2011: 12; Drezner 2007: 45–7). Regulators also resist having their decisions challenged by trade policy considerations (Nicolaïdis 2000: 579; OECD 2013: 89–90). While some societal actors may see the possibility of upgrading domestic protections, it is more common for them to fear the harmonization will reflect the lowest common denominator and thus be deregulatory (e.g., AFL-CIO *et al.* 2014). Thus, each party has a strong preference to have its rule adopted. As a result, regulatory harmonization has distributional implications.

Consequently, the outcome of regulatory harmonization is expected to reflect the distribution of power between the parties (Drezner 2007: 34–5; Krasner 1991: 336). As reviewed in the introduction to this collection (Young 2015), the literature identifies three main power resources in regulatory co-ordination: market size; rule stringency; and regulatory capacity. All three are relative. The larger the foreign market compared to the home market, the greater the costs actors should be willing to incur to gain access to it. When regulations govern product or service-provider characteristics, firms from the party with less stringent rules are normally excluded from the more stringent party's market. Harmonization, therefore, would give them greater market access, which might still be worth it even if the more stringent standard becomes the common one. When regulations govern how things are produced – such as labour and many environmental standards – the adoption of a common regulation yields no increase in market access, but does impose costs on firms in the party with less stringent regulations, which tends to undermine support in the lower-standard country for harmonization. In the context of a PTA negotiation, however, progress on aligning process standards is linked to the conclusion of the agreement, which would offer improved market access for at least some firms. Thus, all regulatory co-ordination in the context of a PTA occurs with the prospect of exclusion.

There is an important caveat to the more stringent product standard conveying bargaining advantage, however. The greater the difference in rule stringency, the greater the costs of adjusting to it are likely to be. It is therefore possible that the expected costs of adjustment might outweigh the anticipated benefits of increased market access (Drezner 2007: 46). In such cases co-ordination will not happen. Thus, greater rule stringency conveys negotiating advantage only up to a point.

The political implications of regulatory capacity are closely related to, but distinct from, those of rule stringency. First, the literature that emphasizes the importance of regulatory capacity (Bach and Newman 2010; Newman and Posner 2015; Posner 2009) highlights the ability to be the first to adopt rules; a unique form of regulatory stringency. Second, regulatory capacity matters in terms of being able to enforce effectively stringent regulations on

THE EUROPEAN UNION AS A GLOBAL REGULATOR?

foreign products and service providers. Regulatory capacity, therefore, reinforces the implications of rule stringency.

Market size, rule stringency and regulatory capacity, therefore, are reinforcing. Moreover, as regulatory co-ordination in PTAs occurs through power-based bargaining with the possibility of exclusion, these regulatory capabilities are expected to be potent (see Young 2015). The EU's large market, generally stringent rules and significant regulatory capacity, therefore, suggest that it should be able to export its rules with respect to most trade partners.

Convergence has many of same dynamics as harmonization, but has received much less attention in the literature. Because convergence implies a less radical change to domestic rules – movement towards another regulation rather than its duplication – the adjustment costs for firms are lower and there is more room for domestic regulators to accommodate domestic considerations. With respect to product and service regulations, if convergence is sufficient for equivalence to be accepted, it can bring the benefits of harmonization to firms, but at a lower cost. It is thus more likely than harmonization (Müller *et al.* 2014: 1109). Nonetheless, as there will still be adjustment costs, the outcome is likely to reflect bargaining power. Convergence is thus more likely than harmonization in general, but it also more likely to occur the greater the EU's relative power.

Where equivalence is accepted, trade is liberalized without adjustment costs for firms or interference with regulators. The literature tends to assume reciprocal equivalence – often called 'mutual recognition' – in which both parties accept that at least some of the other party's rules are equivalent in effect to its own. Establishing that rules are equivalent in effect is demanding, requiring that the parties establish that their regulatory objectives are similar and that their domestic rules are effective in realizing those objectives (Commission 2001: 12; OECD 2013: 100). While firms and regulators tend to favour regulatory co-ordination through equivalence, civic interest groups tend to be concerned that the regulatory objectives are not comparable and/or that the rules are not equally effective, and thus they tend to see establishing equivalence as deregulatory (see, for instance, AFL-CIO *et al.* [2014]). Comparable regulatory capacity is therefore essential, because regulators on both sides need to be able to trust the other to make appropriate regulatory choices (adopt measures equivalent in effect), as well as effectively implement them (WTO 2012: 178–9). Consequently, the EU should establish reciprocal equivalence only with partners with high regulatory capacities.

Equivalence, however, is not necessarily reciprocal. A country with a lower standard may accept another's rule as equivalent, but not vice versa. In such cases, equivalence has the characteristic of unilateral liberalization, and thus is likely only when the more stringent standard country has a much larger market. Such unilateral equivalence, should it occur, should therefore favour the EU.

THE EUROPEAN UNION AS A GLOBAL REGULATOR?

THE EU'S PRACTICE OF REGULATORY CO-ORDINATION

This contribution now turns to the question of what form the EU's regulatory co-ordination has taken in the 'new generation' PTAs it has pursued since the Global Europe strategy was launched, and particularly to what extent has the EU exported its rules through this apparently promising medium. The analysis includes the EU's implemented PTAs with Central America (EU–CA) and South Korea (KOREU); its signed agreements with Canada (the Comprehensive Economic and Trade Agreement [CETA]) and Singapore (EU–S); and its position in the Transatlantic Trade and Investment Partnership (TTIP) negotiations with the United States. It thus considers four of the five PTAs concluded as of the end of 2014 and its most ambitious attempt at regulatory co-ordination. These agreements and negotiations therefore provide an excellent opportunity to assess the extent to which the EU has exported its regulations.

These existing and under-negotiation PTAs involve diverse trade partners. This diversity enables the analysis to consider variation in two key independent variables associated with the form of regulatory co-ordination: relative market size and regulatory capacity (see Table 1). In the light of the relationships between market size and regulatory capacity on the one hand and the forms of regulatory co-ordination on the other, it is possible to develop some, admittedly rather crude, expectations about the character of regulatory co-ordination in the EU's various PTAs. First, convergence (let alone harmonization) is least

Table 1 Pertinent trade partner characteristics

	Economy as a share of EU economy	Government effectiveness (percentile rank, 2012)
Central America	2.0% (2012)	38.0
Singapore	2.3% (2012)	99.5
Canada	8.6% (2013)	95.2
Korea	9.3% (2011)	84.2
United States	98.3% (2013)	90.4

Notes: Relative market size is based on gross national income in purchasing power parity terms as a proportion of the EU's. The Central American economies are aggregated.

The World Bank's 'government effectiveness' is used as a proxy for regulatory capacity. It covers general aspects of public administration, but is a more appropriate as a measure of capacity than 'rule of law,' which focuses on law and order, and 'regulatory quality', which focuses on business-friendliness. Government effectiveness for Central America is the median of the participating states. The average was 42.3 per cent.

Sources: Own calculations based on World Bank, 'World Development Indicators' (available at: http://data.worldbank.org/indicator/NY.GNP.MKTP.PP.CD; accessed 30 July 2014) and 'Worldwide Governance Indicators' (available at http://www.govindicators.org; accessed 30 July 2014).

likely in the context of TTIP, given the comparable size of the two economies, and most likely with respect to Central America and Singapore. Second, where there is convergence (even harmonization), it is likely to be towards the EU's rule, given its greater economic weight than the other trade partners. Third, the dominant form of co-ordination with the United States (US) will be through reciprocal equivalence, but this will not be part of the PTA with Central America.

Exporting which rules?

As this is a preliminary investigation of whether the EU exports its regulations through bilateral PTAs, the analysis focuses on those regulations that the EU should be most likely to export. Two criteria were used to identify the most likely cases: (1) those regulations that the EU is widely regarded as exporting in other contexts (motive); and (2) those EU regulations that are regarded as particularly stringent, thus lending negotiating leverage (means). There is, not surprisingly, considerable overlap between regulations meeting these two criteria.

The EU's product standards are considered to be particularly stringent (Bradford 2012; Vogel 2012), and the Commission (1996:4; 2006: 5, 9) has emphasized encouraging others to adopt EU standards as a means of liberalizing trade. It also has robust domestic rules governing financial services and has engaged actively in international co-operation on such rules (Posner 2009; Quaglia 2013, 2014). The EU's competition regime is recognized as one of the world's most sophisticated (Global Competition Review 2013: 4) and the EU has been particularly active in promoting international competition co-operation (Meunier and Nicolaïdis 2006: 910; Woolcock 2007: 9). The EU has some of the most stringent protections of personal data (Greenleaf 2012: 70; Newman 2008) and has prompted others to follow suit (Newman 2008: 6; Zielonka 2008: 474). The EU has also sought to promote both environmental and labour standards through PTAs (Meunier and Nicolaïdis 2006: 907; Zielonka 2008: 480). The EU is regarded as the world's most stringent environmental regulator (Vogel 2012: 4–5). Europe is also considered to have stringent labour provisions, although these are primarily at the national level (ETUC 2006; Vaughan-Whitehead 2014). These represent a diverse array of regulations that the EU can reasonably be expected to be trying to export and for which its power resources should be considerable.

Assessing co-ordination

As regulatory co-ordination entails reducing the adverse effects of existing measures, by definition it implies that at least one party must do something it otherwise would not – change its rules or accept the equivalence of the other party's measures. For these purposes the commitments in the PTA must go beyond those the parties have already accepted under the WTO or in other multilateral agreements. Thus, commitments to use international standards are considered co-ordination only if they go substantially beyond the obligation in the Technical Barriers to Trade (TBT) Agreement (Art. 2.4) or the Sanitary and Phystosanitary (SPS) Agreement (Art. 3.1). Likewise, commitments to enforce existing rules and implement accepted multilateral obligations are not considered co-ordination, but requirements to ratify agreements are.

For regulatory co-ordination to be meaningful in a real world sense, the parties have to do what they have agreed to do. This is generally considered more likely if an agreement creates a legal obligation to act. Provisions convey greater obligation the more unambiguously they define conduct that they explicitly require or prohibit (Abbott *et al.* 2000: 401; Horn *et al.* 2009: 13). Thus, a commitment that the parties must adopt a particular piece of legislation with specified content within a set period of time would convey high obligation. Provisions that call on the parties to co-operate in order to reduce regulatory barriers conveys low obligation. Where provisions convey high obligation, I also consider whether they are subject to binding dispute resolution. If they are not, it weakens the obligation (Abbott *et al.* 2000: 401; Horn *et al.* 2009: 13). In addition to whether a commitment is strong or weak, it may also be limited in that it applies to relatively few, specified measures within a policy area.

For the signed agreements, the analysis is based on textual analysis of the agreements themselves.[1] As the Commission's initial negotiating position in the TTIP talks has been leaked,[2] it is possible to assess what the EU's aspirations are, irrespective of whether it will be able to realize them. Given that the negotiations are a form of strategic interaction, the EU's positions are assumed to represent what it considers to be the best possible realistic outcome. In this sense the EU's negotiating positions present a maximalist version (from the EU's perspective) of a likely agreement.

Goods: all about cars

Addressing regulatory obstacles to trade in goods is, to a significant extent, the *raison d'etre* of the EU's new generation of PTAs, so one would expect regulatory co-operation to figure prominently in the agreements. None of the agreements' general provisions on technical barriers to trade, however, go much beyond the TBT Agreement's obligation to use international standards, except where they would be an ineffective or inappropriate means for the fulfilment of the legitimate objectives. Regulatory co-ordination with respect to TBTs is generally surprisingly limited.

The striking exception is with respect to regulations affecting motor vehicles. The EU–Korea agreement goes the furthest. It lists domestic rules that each party considers to be already equivalent to specific standards of the United Nation's Economic Commission for Europe (UNECE), and specifies domestic regulations to be 'harmonised' with specific UNECE standards within five years (Annex 2-C Art. 3(a)(iii)). Significantly, Korea must modify 29 of its

THE EUROPEAN UNION AS A GLOBAL REGULATOR?

regulations to only one by the EU. Moreover, as the EU exercises considerable influence over UNECE standards (Porter 2011: 80), in this instance the EU might be exporting its regulations indirectly. Singapore agreed to treat EU or UNECE motor vehicle regulations as equivalent to its own (Annex 2-B; Art. 3.5). Canada, too, has agreed to accept UNECE standards as equivalent to its own, but on a much more limited basis. CETA specifies 17 UNECE standards that Canada accepts as equivalent, although only three of these were new (Canada 2013: 9) and no modifications to Canada's regulations are envisaged. These provisions are all subject to dispute settlement. The EU's ambition in TTIP is greater, seeking for each party to accept the other's safety standards as equivalent (mutual recognition), with the 'methodological presumption' being that they are (Commission 2013c: 1). Motor vehicles thus stand out as a sector in which the EU's regulatory co-ordination has been particularly intense, but even here, with the possible exception of Korea, the EU has not exported its rules.

Regulatory co-ordination on food safety has been more limited than with respect to motor vehicles. The agreements with Central America and Singapore do not go beyond the SPS Agreement's provision that the parties 'may' recognize the other's rules as equivalent (Art. 150 and 5.14.1 respectively). The EU–Korea FTA focuses on developing common understandings on the application of international food safety standards (Art. 5.6(a)). Canada and the US, however, both concluded veterinary equivalence agreements (VEAs) with the EU in the 1990s, which specify which standards are considered equivalent, as well as ones where some modification is required. CETA 'up-dates' the existing VEA (Canada 2013: 11) and includes a list of measures that are considered equivalent in effect as is or with conditions (SPS Art. 7 and Annex V), and thus goes further than the other PTAs. The Commission (2013e: 2), likewise, envisages incorporating and building upon is 1998 VEA with the US in TTIP, but it stresses the importance of the 'right of each Party to appraise and manage risks in accordance with the level of protection it deems appropriate . . .' (Commission 2013e: 1). With respect to food safety, rather than seeking to export its rules, the EU has sought to fend off demands from the US that the EU ease some of its food safety measures. Thus, the EU is not seeking to export its food safety rules through PTAs; rather, it has kept co-operation intentionally limited in order to preserve domestic regulatory autonomy.

Looking across these agreements, it is striking how limited regulatory co-ordination with respect to goods has been. Harmonization, and thus the pure export of EU rules, is entirely absent. The closest the EU comes to exporting its rules is South Korea's agreement to modify some of its motor vehicle regulations to align with EU-influenced international standards. It also exerted influence, albeit without rule export, in getting Singapore to unilaterally accept EU standards. With respect to food safety, the EU seems to be more interested in preserving its rules than exporting them. This raises the question about how much the EU is even trying to export its regulations.

Financial services regulation: preserving prudence

As the EU is a leading exporter of services and a dominant player in the regulation of financial services, one would expect financial service liberalization to be high on its bilateral trade agenda. It certainly is, but the EU's main focus has been on liberalizing market access and securing national treatment. When it comes to domestic regulation the EU's PTAs emphasize domestic autonomy, with each of the agreements including a 'prudential carve-out' (EU–CA Art. 195; KOREU Art. 7.38; CETA 15 Art. 15.1; EU–S Art. 8.50.1). The agreements with Central America and Singapore call for the use of international standards for financial regulation, but these are only a 'best endeavour' clauses (Art. 196.3 and Art. 8.50.4), and in the case of Central America no specific standards are mentioned, and so convey low obligation. The Commission's (2014) proposal for regulatory co-ordination in financial services in TTIP goes further. Nonetheless, it emphasizes mutual reliance, equivalence and substituted compliance, rather than any form of convergence. As of the end of 2014, the US was resisting including financial services in the negotiations, and the EU did not include financial services in its initial market access offer on services (*Bridges* 2014a; 2014b). Thus, the EU has not sought to export its prudential supervision rules through any of the existing or planned PTAs considered here.

Competition policy: levelling the playing field

The EU put a heavy emphasis on competition provisions in its pre-Global Europe PTAs (Horn *et al.* 2009: 43), and competition policy has continued to receive attention in its new generation PTAs. The form of co-ordination, however, has differed significantly across partners. The partner's regulatory capacity seems to be the prime determinant of the EU's approach to the co-ordination of competition policies, but there is little export of the EU's approach.

Of the PTAs considered here, only the one with Central America involves countries that did not have competition laws before the agreement. The association agreement requires those parties that do not already have competition laws to adopt 'comprehensive competition laws', which 'effectively address' specified anti-competitive practices, and to establish a competition authority within a specified time frame (Art. 279). These requirements, however, are explicitly excluded from binding dispute resolution (Art. 283), which weakens the obligation. The agreements with Korea and Singapore, by contrast, require the maintenance of existing competition laws and authorities (Art. 11 and Art. 12). CETA (19 Art. X-01) requires the parties to take 'appropriate measures to proscribe anti-competitive business conduct'. The Commission's (2013b: 2) proposal for competition policy in TTIP includes a similar provision. Significantly, the agreements with Korea and Canada and planned with the US rest

THE EUROPEAN UNION AS A GLOBAL REGULATOR?

extensively on competition co-operation agreements that they had concluded with the EU prior to the launch of the PTA negotiations. Thus, weak convergence occurs only in the form of institution (and capacity) building in the least developed of the considered partners.

Data protection: limited convergence

The EU's 1995 Data Privacy Directive established strict and comprehensive data protection requirements and prohibits the transfer of data to countries whose data protection regimes have not been recognized as 'adequate' by the Commission (Newman 2008: 32). Given the importance of data flows in global commerce, one would expect the EU to seek to export data protection through PTAs. To an extent it does promote convergence through its PTAs, but much less thoroughly than might be expected.

For a start, although the EU itself has a comprehensive privacy regime, the data protection provisions in its PTAs have tended to be sector specific. Only in the EU–Central America PTA is there a general commitment to protecting privacy, but this commitment has both a low level of obligation and specifies international standards of protection, rather than European ones (Art. 34.1). The EU's PTAs with Canada, Korea and Singapore have only sectoral provisions.[3]

All four agreements have provisions with respect to e-commerce, which refer to international standards. While the Korea and Singapore agreements state that 'the development of electronic commerce must be fully compatible with international standards of data protection' (Art. 7.48.2 and Art. 8.57.4), the Central America PTA (Art. 201.2) and CETA (18 Art. X-03) are much less definitive. The e-commerce clauses thus tend to be low in terms of obligation and reference international standards.

The provisions with respect to data protection in financial services in the Central America, Korea and Singapore PTAs, however, are more robust. The PTAs with Central America and Singapore (Art. 198.2; Art. 8.54.2) state that the parties 'shall adopt or maintain' 'adequate' or 'appropriate' (respectively) safeguards to protect privacy. The provisions in the EU's PTA with Korea are somewhat more precise. It specifies a timeframe for adopting 'adequate safeguards' that are meant to protect fundamental rights in specified international agreements (Art. 7.43). In all of these cases there is a degree of convergence towards the EU, but the sectoral approach to protecting privacy and the emphasis on international standards means that these obligations are a far cry from harmonization.

Strikingly, the EU has sought actively to exclude data protection from the remit of the TTIP negotiations, at least in part because of concerns that the talks would put downward pressure on European standards, which the Commission has been unwilling to countenance (Fontanella-Khan 2013). The EU's export of data privacy standards through PTAs has thus been very limited.

THE EUROPEAN UNION AS A GLOBAL REGULATOR?

Environmental and labour market regulation: preventing back sliding

All the PTAs analysed here include binding obligations to not lower environmental or labour standards in order to attract trade or investment (EU–CA Art. 291.2; KOREU Art. 13.7; CETA 24 Art. 4; 25 Art. X.5; EU–S Art. 13.12; Commission 2013f: para 11). Such 'no rollback' clauses preclude the parties doing something they might otherwise do, but they do not entail any reduction in existing differences, and so does not constitute co-ordination.

The PTAs also address the parties' multilateral obligations. In most of the PTAs the provisions require only the effective implementation of already accepted multilateral standards (KOREU Art. 13.4 and 13.7; CETA 24 Art. 3; EU–S Art. 13.6; Commission 2013f: para 11). As these provisions refer to existing obligations, they do not constitute co-ordination. The EU-Central America PTA, however, calls for convergence with respect to environmental regulations, with all of the parties undertaking to ratify two specific multilateral environmental agreements by the time the agreement enters into force (Art. 287). This requirement, however, is explicitly excluded from binding dispute settlement (Art. 284.4), thus weakening the obligation. The regulatory co-ordination in the EU–Singapore PTA (Art. 13.3), by contrast, is stronger with respect to labour standards than environmental protection, although the call for 'continued and sustained efforts towards ratifying and effectively implementing' the core labour standards has low obligation and so suggests only weak convergence. For the most part, therefore, the EU's PTAs largely preserve existing differences with respect to environmental and labour regulation, with weak and limited convergence with respect to the environment in the EU–Central America PTA and labour standards in the EU–Singapore agreement.

THE LIMITS OF CO-ORDINATION

The striking takeaway from this analysis is the total absence of harmonization based on EU rules. Across a wide range of regulations with a variety of partners, there is strikingly little regulatory co-ordination in general (see Table 2). The only clear example of convergence is with respect to some automobile standards in the EU–Korea PTA. All other examples of convergence are either weak, in that the obligation is heavily qualified or excluded from binding dispute settlement, or limited, in that it applies to relatively few of the relevant measures, or both. Moreover, what convergence there is is overwhelmingly based on international standards, rather than European rules. Thus, there is scant evidence of the EU exporting its regulations through new generation PTAs. As these should be relatively easy cases for the EU to export its rules – in that regulatory co-ordination is a focus of these PTAs and the EU enjoys a considerable power advantage with each of its partners other than the US – this finding is contrary to expectations derived from the literature on the EU as a global regulator.

This puzzling finding provokes the question: why is the EU not exporting its rules through PTAs? In particular, why has the EU not exported it regulations in

these agreements when it had in earlier agreements. A satisfactory answer is beyond the scope of this contribution; however, it does suggest a plausible explanation.

First, as discussed previously, regulatory co-operation in previous PTAs, contrary to common perceptions, exceptionally rarely involved the other party adopting EU rules. In the case of technical regulations, convergence on international standards was far more common (Piermartini and Budetta 2009: Annex 2). Even with respect to labour standards, which figure prominently in some accounts of the EU promoting its rules through trade (see, for example, Meunier and Nicolaïdis [2006: 913]), the EU emphasized international standards and did so through non-binding obligations (Postnikov and Bastiaens 2014: 924). The exceptional examples of actual EU rule export, therefore, are confined to the countries that have applied or are intending to apply for membership of the EU. This corrective refines the puzzle somewhat. It is less 'What is exceptional about the new generation PTAs?' than 'Why has the EU not exported its rules more generally?'

The existing literature on regulatory co-operation suggests three possible explanations for why the EU has not exported its rules:

1) obdurate bargaining by the other party whittles the EU down from its ambitious objectives;
2) the EU pursues only modest objectives, anticipating that ambitious objectives would jeopardize an agreement; and
3) the EU pursues modest objectives that reflect a compromise among competing internal preferences.

Distinguishing between these alternative explanations is bedevilled by the problem of observational equivalence. Unpicking the different explanations adequately would entail extensive further research, which is beyond the scope of this contribution, but which would a fruitful line of further enquiry.

Isolating the first explanation would require analysis of the EU's negotiating objectives and contrasting them with the outcomes. Identifying the EU's negotiating objectives, however, is not generally possible other than through interviews, with their attendant problems. The Forum of the Caribbean Group of African, Caribbean and Pacific (ACP) States (CARIFORUM) negotiator's account of the Economic and Partnership Agreement (EPA) negotiations with the EU, however, suggests that even objectively less-powerful actors can scale back the EU's ambitions (Bernal 2013: 45). This account, however, hinges on the EU's negotiating leverage being undermined by its desire for a success in its new but troubled EPA policy. Nonetheless, this account lends credence to the possibility of resistance by a negotiating partner causing the EU to back away from ambitious objectives. The very limited nature of regulatory co-ordination across an array of issues and variety of partners considered here, however, suggest that this is not the most likely explanation. Moreover, even to the extent that this explanation holds, it prompts the question: why do the EU's partners resist regulatory co-ordination?

THE EUROPEAN UNION AS A GLOBAL REGULATOR?

The second, and more plausible, explanation acknowledges that bilateral trade negotiations are a form of strategic interaction and that the parties avoid making demands that would jeopardize an agreement that would be valuable, even if suboptimal. This is a subtly distinct argument from the first because it rests on the complexities of regulatory co-ordination rather than straight bargaining power. There are examples in the EU-as-a-global-regulator literature of the EU moderating its position in multilateral negotiations in order to avoid being isolated and thus being able to exert more influence (Groen *et al.* 2012: 185; Mair 2008: 21–2). The EU's leaked TTIP negotiating positions also suggest that the EU is moderating its position in anticipation of difficulties. As discussed above, the EU held off on tabling an offer on financial services given opposition from US regulators to discussion of regulatory co-ordination. Moreover, the Commission (2013d: 1) thinks that the American and European approaches to regulating chemicals are too different to try to establish equivalence in the short term. Thus, the EU has tempered its efforts at regulatory co-ordination in the light the political and administrative challenges. Of course, given their parity, the EU is more likely to moderate its objectives with the US than with any other partner, so that observation cannot be assumed to hold for the other cases; nonetheless, it is a more than plausible explanation.

The third possible explanation for why the EU might have modest negotiating objectives is that internal differences cause the EU to adopt a lowest common denominator positions. Problems of internal agreement have certainly been identified in the literature as contributing to weak negotiating positions, particularly as high decision thresholds strengthen the hands of those most opposed to change (Groen *et al.* 2012: 182; Meunier 2005: 67). The problem of internal agreement, however, largely goes away when the EU is seeking to export existing common rules, even in areas of mixed competence where all member states would have to ratify an agreement (Kelemen and Vogel 2010: 431; Young 2002: 158). This is the case with respect to most of the regulatory issues considered here. The only partial exception has been with respect to labour and environmental standards, where there has been long-standing tension among the member states about the use of coercion versus persuasion to promote them (Ahnlid 2005: 136; Young 2007: 805). Even here, the opposition of some member state governments has been tactical, concerned that aggressively pushing environmental and labour standards would make developing countries less willing to engage. The EU's high decision threshold has led to the more moderate emphasis on persuasion becoming the norm. This explanation, however, applies to only a small part of the EU's negotiating agenda and at least partially reflects concerns about making agreements unpalatable to its partners.

Although ostensibly different, a common thread underpins each of these explanations; the domestic political complexity of regulatory co-ordination. The domestic political costs associated with harmonizing to EU rules provide a motivation for the EU's partners to bargain hard in the first explanation. In the second explanation, concerns that opposition to the costs associated with

THE EUROPEAN UNION AS A GLOBAL REGULATOR?

harmonization to (or convergence with) EU rules would jeopardize an agreement beneficial to European firms prompts the EU to moderate its demands. In the third explanation, such concerns inform the positions of some, but only some, member states, undermining EU unity, leading to a moderate position. Whichever the precise pathway, the domestic costs of adjustment implied by regulatory co-ordination are at the root of the EU's limited export of its rules through PTAs.

The exception of harmonization in the EU's agreements with some neighbouring countries is consistent with this account. With respect to countries in its neighbourhood, there are strong political reasons driving the EU's over-all policy (Sedelmeier 2015), and regulatory approximation is a necessary feature of accession. Thus, not promoting harmonization is not an issue. For the EU's partners, the incentives of enhanced access to the EU's large market and the prospect of eventual membership, assuming it is credible, can make bearing even high costs of adjustment worthwhile (Sedelmeier 2015).[4] Such an overwhelming incentive to incur adjustment costs, however, is exceptionally rare. It is absent even among the Central American countries, the weakest partners considered here. This is particularly the case as they must be concerned that aligning with European rules would increase divergence with the regulations of the US, by far their more important export market.[5] The complexities of domestic regulatory politics therefore mean that the EU does not, and to a significant extent does not try to, export its regulations bilaterally much beyond its borders.

CONCLUSIONS

This analysis of four of the earliest of the EU's new generation of preferential trade agreements – those with Canada, Central America, Singapore and South Korea – and the EU's position in the most ambitious – TTIP – reveals categorically that the EU does not export its regulations through preferential trade agreements. Agreement to reduce existing regulatory differences – regulatory co-ordination – is rare. Where there is regulatory co-ordination it occurs through either convergence on the basis of international standards (not EU rules) or through the acceptance of equivalence, which implies no rule change. This observation does not mean that the EU has not reduced regulatory barriers through its PTAs, nor that regulatory co-ordination occurs only in PTAs, but it does mean that, contrary to expectations, the EU's formidable trade power is not leveraged through the new generation PTAs to export its regulations to its trade partners.

The critical qualifier of the generally low degree of regulatory co-ordination aside, the variation across the partners broadly coincides with expectations. The greatest degree of convergence is by the weakest partner – Central America – and the EU is not even seeking it with the most powerful – the US. In addition, in each case of convergence, the partner has moved towards the EU's position. Further, reciprocal equivalence has been pursued only among parties with comparable regulatory capacities. Unilateral acceptance of

THE EUROPEAN UNION AS A GLOBAL REGULATOR?

equivalence has always been by the weaker, other party. Thus, the existing literature does a decent job of explaining the form of regulatory co-ordination should it occur, but offers little insight into whether it will occur.

This contribution argues that the reason the EU has not exported it rules, even as it has sought to export its goods and services, hinges on the complex domestic politics of regulatory co-ordination. Regulatory co-ordination, because it implies at least one party changing its rules, conveys anticipated costs for firms, consumers and regulators. Consequently, there tends to be substantial opposition. The impact of such opposition is amplified by the *status quo* bias in the policy process, even more so when there are many veto players. Consequently, it is only when the expected benefits are truly substantial that there is sufficient support for incurring cost in pursuit of the gain that regulatory co-ordination can be agreed. Thus, it is only those states that aspire to join the EU that have been willing to accept PTAs that export EU rules. For others the gains do not outweigh the costs. This dynamic is sufficiently powerful, this contribution suggests, that the EU has generally not sought to export its rules for fear that doing so would jeopardize trade liberalization.

Biographical note: Alasdair Young is professor of international affairs and Jean Monnet Chair in the Sam Nunn School of International Affairs, Georgia Institute of Technology. He is also chair of the European Union Studies Association (2015–17).

ACKNOWLEDGEMENTS

This contribution is part of a wider project that has been funded with support from the European Commission (Jean Monnet Chair 2012-3121). It reflects the views only of the author, and the Commission cannot be held responsible for any use which may be made of the information contained herein. I am grateful to Yujia He and Tom Hazzard for their research assistance and to the Sam Nunn School for funding it. Earlier versions of this contribution were presented at the European Union Studies Association Conference, Baltimore, 9–11 May 2013; the International Studies Association Convention, 26–29 Toronto March 2014; the 'Regulatory Power Europe?' Jean Monnet Chair Workshop, Georgia Institute of Technology, 18–19 April 2014; and the Workshop on 'European Regulation: Comparative and International Perspectives,' University of California, Berkeley, 23–25 April 2014. I am grateful to all of the workshop participants, Tom Doleys and Robert Wolfe and two anonymous referees for their comments. I assert sole ownership of all errors and omissions.

THE EUROPEAN UNION AS A GLOBAL REGULATOR?

NOTES

1 Consolidated CETA Text, 26 September 2014, available at http://trade.ec.europa. eu/doclib/html/152806.htm (accessed 15 December 2014). Agreement establishing an association between Central America, on the one hand, and the European Union and its member states', text available at http://trade.ec.europa.eu/doclib/ press/index.cfm?id=689 (accessed 31 July 2014). Free Trade Agreement between the European Union and its Member States, of the one part, and the Republic of Korea, of the other part, *Official Journal*, L127/6, 14 May 2011. Text of the EU– Singapore Free Trade Agreement, 20 September 2013, available at http://trade.ec. europa.eu/doclib/press/index.cfm?id=961 (accessed 15 December 2014).
2 Available on Inside US Trade's website at http://insidetrade.com/Inside-Trade-General/Public-Content-World-Trade-Online/leaked-document-details-eu-goals-for-ttip-chapters-ahead-of-first-negotiating-session/menu-id-896.html (accessed 18 July 2014).
3 In 2001 the Commission accepted the adequacy of Canada's Personal Information Protection and Electronic Documents Act.
4 Comments by a senior diplomat form an eastern European country, Atlanta, 3 March 2014.
5 According to their WTO trade profiles, of the Central American states the EU was a more important export destination than the US for only Panama (exports to the EU in 2013 were 30 per cent higher than to the US). For the others the US was a much more important export market, ranging from accounting for 70 per cent more exports from Honduras to 11 times more for El Salvador. The trade profiles are accessible via the WTO's website at https://www.wto.org/english/thewto_e/whatis_e/tif_ e/org6_e.htm (accessed 10 April 2015). Concern about increasing regulatory divergence with the US also restricted Canada's willingness to pursue regulatory co-ordination with the EU (comments by a Canadian diplomat, Washington, DC, 26 January 2015).

REFERENCES

Abbott, K.W., Keohane, R.O., Moravcsik, A., Slaughter, A.-M. and Snidal, D. (2000) 'The concept of legalization' *International Organization* 54(3): 401–19.
AFL-CIO *et al* (2014) 'Concerning the Trans-Atlantic Trade and Investment Partnership', Available at http://www.greenbusinessnetwork.org/take-policy-action/item/ 986-concerning-the-trans-atlantic-trade-and-investment-partnership.html (accessed 17 August 2014).
Ahnlid, A. (2005) 'Setting the global trade agenda: the European Union and the launch of the Doha Round', in O. Elgström and C. Jönsson (eds), *European Union Negotiations: Processes, Networks and Institutions*, London: Routledge, pp. 130–47.
Bach, D. and Newman, A.L. (2010) 'Governing lipitor and lipstick: capacity, sequencing, and power in international pharmaceutical and cosmetics regulation', *Review of International Political Economy* 17(4): 665–95.
Bernal, R.L. (2013) *Globalization, Trade and Economic Development: The CARI-FORUM-EU Economic Partnership Agreement*, Basingstoke: Palgrave Macmillan.
Bradford, A. (2012) 'The Brussels effect', *Northwestern University Law Review* 107(1): 1–68.
Bridges (2014a) 'EU–US trade talks advance, amid charged election climate,' *Bridges* 18(19), 28 May, available at http://www.ictsd.org/bridges-news/bridges-africa/news/ eu-us-trade-talks-advance-amid-charged-election-climate (accessed May 2015).
Bridges (2014b) 'TTIP negotiators advance technical work as EU begins leadership transitions,' *Bridges* 18(27), 24 July, available at http://www.ictsd.org/bridges-

news/bridges/news/ttip-negotiators-advance-technical-work-as-eu-begins-leadership (accessed May 2015).

Büthe, T. and Mattli, W. (2011) *The New Global Rulers: The Privatization of Regulation in the World Economy*, Princeton, NJ: Princeton University Press.

Canada (2013) 'Technical summary of final negotiated outcomes: Canada–European Union Comprehensive Economic and Trade Agreement: agreement-in-principle', available at http://www.actionplan.gc.ca/sites/default/files/pdfs/ceta-technicalsumm ary.pdf (accessed 23 July 2014).

Commission (1996) 'The Global Challenge of International Trade: A Market Access Strategy for the European Union,' COM(96) 53 final, 14 February.

Commission (2001) 'Implementing policy for external trade in the fields of standards and conformity assessment: a tool box of instruments', *SEC(2001) 1570*, 28 September, Brussels: Commission of the European Communities.

Commission (2006) 'Global Europe: competing in the world', *COM(2006) 567 final*, 4 October, Brussels: Commission of the European Communities.

Commission (2013a) 'Trade, growth and jobs: contribution from the Commission to the February 2013 European Council Debate on trade, growth and jobs', Brussels: Commission of the European Communities.

Commission (2013b) 'Initial position paper: anti-trust & mergers, government influence and subsidies', 19 June, Brussels: Commission of the European Communities.

Commission (2013c) 'Annex I: initial position paper: motor vehicles in TTIP', 20 June, Brussels: Commission of the European Communities.

Commission (2013d) 'Annex II: initial position paper: chemicals in TTIP', 20 June, Brussels: Commission of the European Communities.

Commission (2013e) 'EU initial position paper on SPS matters for the TTIP negotiations', 20 June, Brussels: Commission of the European Communities.

Commission (2013f) 'EU initial position paper on trade and sustainable development', 20 June, Brussels: Commission of the European Communities.

Commission (2014) 'Regulatory co-operation on financial regulation in TTIP: text to be circulated to the US during TTIP negotiations on 10–14 March 2014', 5 March, Brussels: Commission of the European Communities, available at http://corporateeurope.org/sites/default/files/attachments/regulatory_coop_fs_-_ec_prop_march_2014-2_0.pdf, (accessed 18 July 2014).

De Gucht, K. (2010) 'Speaking points: future trade policy', European Parliament Committee on International Trade, 22 June.

Drezner, D.W. (2007) *All Politics is Global: Explaining International Regulatory Regimes*, Princeton, NJ: Princeton University Press.

ETUC (2006) 'European social model', available at http://www.etuc.org/european-social-model, (accessed 15 December 2014).

Fontanella-Khan, J. (2013) 'Data protection ruled out of EU-US trade talks', *Financial Times*, 4 November.

García, M. (2013) 'From idealism to realism? EU Preferential Trade Agreement Policy', *Journal of Contemporary European Research* 9(4): 521–41.

Global Competition Review (2013) *Rating Enforcement 2013*, London: Law Business Research.

Greenleaf, G. (2012) 'The Influence of European data privacy standards outside Europe: implications for globalization of Convention 108', *International Data Privacy Law* 2(2): 68–92.

Groen, L., Niemann, A. and Oberthür, S. (2012) 'The EU as a global leader? The Copenhagen and Cancun UN climate change negotiations', *Journal of Contemporary European Research* 8(2): 173–91.

Horn, H., Mavroidis, P.C. and Sapir, A. (2009) *Beyond the WTO? An Anatomy of EU and US Preferential Trade Agreements*, (Bruegel Blueprint Series, volume VII), Brussels: Bruegel.

Kelemen, R.D. and Vogel, D. (2010) 'Trading places: the role of the United States and the European Union in international environmental politics', *Comparative Political Studies* 43(4): 427–56.

Koenig-Archibugi, M. (2010) 'Global regulation', in R. Baldwin, M. Cave and D. Lodge (eds), *The Oxford Handbook of Regulation*, Oxford: Oxford University Press, pp. 406–33.

Krasner, S.D. (1991) 'Global communications and national power: life on the Pareto frontier', *World Politics* 43(3): 336–66.

Mair, M.L. (2008) 'The regulatory state goes global: EU participation in international food standard-setting by the Codex Alimentarius Commission', Paper presented at the GARNET conference on 'The European Union in International Affairs,' Institute for European Studies, Vrije Universiteit, Brussels, 24–26 April.

Meunier, S. (2005) *Trading Voices: The European Union in International Commercial Negotiations*, Princeton, NJ: Princeton University Press.

Meunier, S. and Nicolaïdis, K. (2006) 'The European Union as a conflicted trade power', *Journal of European Public Policy* 13(6): 906–25.

Müller, P. and Falkner, G. (2014) 'The EU as a policy exporter? The conceptual framework', in G. Falkner and P. Müller (eds), *EU Policies in a Global Perspective: Shaping or Taking International Regimes?* London: Routledge.

Müller, P., Kudrna, Z. and Falkner, G. (2014) 'EU–global interactions: policy export, import, promotion and protection', *Journal of European Public Policy* 21(8): 1102–19.

Newman, A. (2008) *Protectors of Privacy: Regulating Personal Data in the Global Economy*, Ithaca, NY: Cornell University Press.

Newman, A.L. and Posner, E. (2015) 'Putting the EU in its place: influence strategies and the global regulatory context', *Journal of European Public Policy*, doi: 10.1080/13501763.2015.1046901.

Nicolaïdis, K. (2000) 'Regulatory cooperation and managed mutual recognition: elements of a strategic model', in G.A. Bermann, M. Herdegen and P.L. Lindseth (eds), *Transatlantic Regulatory Co-operation: Legal Problems and Political Perspectives*, Oxford: Oxford University Press, pp. 571–600.

OECD (2013) *International Regulatory Co-operation: Addressing Global Challenges*, Paris: Organization for Economic Cooperation and Development.

Piermartini, R. and Budetta, M. (2009) 'A mapping of regional rules on technical barriers to trade,' in A. Estevadeordal, K. Suominen and R. Teh (eds), *Regional Rules in the Global Trading System*, Cambridge: Cambridge University Press, pp. 250–315.

Porter, T. (2011) 'Transnational policy paradigm change and conflict in the harmonization of vehicle safety and accounting standards', in G. Skogstad (ed.), *Policy Paradigms: Transnationalism and Domestic Politics*, Toronto: University of Toronto Press, pp. 64–90.

Posner, E. (2009) 'Making rules for global finance: transatlantic regulatory cooperation at the turn of the millennium', *International Organization* 63(4): 665–99.

Postnikov, E. and Bastiaens, I. (2014) 'Does dialogue work? The effectiveness of labor standards in EU preferential trade agreements', *Journal of European Public Policy* 21(6): 923–40.

Quaglia, L. (2013) 'The European Union, the USA and international standard setting by regulatory fora in finance', *New Political Economy*, available at http://dx.doi.org/10.1080/13563467.2013.796449 (accessed 13 May 2013).

Quaglia, L. (2014) 'The European Union, the USA and international standard setting by regulatory fora in finance,' *New Political Economy* 19(3): 427–44.

THE EUROPEAN UNION AS A GLOBAL REGULATOR?

Sedelmeier, U. (2015) 'Enlargement: constituent policy and tool for external governance', in H. Wallace, M.A. Pollack and A.R. Young (eds), *Policy-Making in the European Union*, 7th edn, Oxford: Oxford University Press, pp. 407–35.

Sierra Club (2013) 'The Transatlantic Free Trade Agreement: what is at stake for communities and the environment', Washington, DC: Sierra Club.

Stoler, A.L. (2011) 'TBT and SPS measures in practice', J.-P. Chauffour and J.-C. Maur (eds), *Preferential Trade Agreement Policies for Development: A Handbook*, Washington, DC: The World Bank, pp. 217–34.

Vaughan-Whitehead, D. (2014) 'Why the European Social Model is still relevant', 19 March, available at http://www.ilo.org/global/about-the-ilo/newsroom/comment-analysis/WCMS_238253/lang–en/index.htm (accessed 15 December 2014).

Vogel, D. (2012) *The Politics of Precaution: Regulating Health, Safety, and Environmental Risks in Europe and the United States*, Princeton, NJ: Princeton University Press.

Woolcock, S. (2007) 'European Union policy towards free trade agreements,' *ECIPE Working Paper 3/2007*, Brussels: European Centre for International Political Economy.

WTO (2011) *World Trade Report 2011: The WTO and Preferential Trade Agreements: From Co-Existence to Coherence*, Geneva: World Trade Organisation.

WTO (2012) *World Trade Report 2012: Trade and Public Policies: A Closer Look at Non-Tariff Measures in the 21st Century*, Geneva: World Trade Organisation.

Young, A.R. (2002) *Extending European Cooperation: The European Union and the 'New' International Trade Agenda*, Manchester: Manchester University Press.

Young, A.R. (2007) 'Negotiating with diminished expectations: the European Union and the Doha development agenda', in D. Lee and R. Wilkinson (eds), *The WTO after Hong Kong: Progress in, and Prospects for, the Doha Development Agenda*, London: Routledge, pp. 119–36.

Young, A.R. (2015) 'The European Union as a global regulator? Context and comparison', *Journal of European Public Policy*, doi: 10.1080/13501763.2015.1046902.

Young, A.R. and Peterson, J. (2006) 'The EU and the new trade politics', *Journal of European Public Policy* 13(6): 795–814.

Young, A.R. and Peterson, J. (2014) *Parochial Global Europe: 21st Century Trade Politics*, Oxford: Oxford University Press.

Zielonka, J. (2008) 'Europe as a global actor: empire by example?' *International Affairs* 84(3): 471–84.

THE EUROPEAN UNION AS A GLOBAL REGULATOR?

advocacy for greater international co-operation on reducing greenhouse gas emissions, there is a distinct gap between advocacy and tangible influence. Such a gap was clearly on display at the 2009 Copenhagen United Nations (UN) Climate Conference, where, despite its aspirations, the EU was largely sidelined by the United States (US) and China. Second, the interests of the countries that shut the EU out at Copenhagen and had long-resisted its appeals for multilateral action on aviation emissions within the ICAO did not change. Third, climate change negotiations are characterized by power-based bargaining where there is not generally the prospect for excluding non-complying firms from the EU's large market, which means that the costs of no agreement are more pronounced for the leader than for laggards (Young 2015). Fourth, whereas the EU is an official party to both the Kyoto Protocol and the United National Framework Convention on Climate Change, it is not a member of the International Civil Aviation Organization. Such a lack of membership is often associated in the literature with reduced influence. For all of these reasons, aviation emissions regulation is a hard case for EU influence. Thus, even getting the issue on ICAO's agenda is a manifestation of influence, though the real test will be whether the ICAO discussions result in a meaningful agreement.

The contribution makes three related arguments. First, it demonstrates that by deciding to include the entirety of all flights to and from EU airports in its Emissions Trading System (ETS), the EU raised the cost of no agreement for foreign airlines and thereby contributed to a change in the preferences of its negotiating partners and the ensuing inclusion of the issue on ICAO's agenda. The timing of the EU's move and ICAO's decision suggest this was the decisive factor. Consequently, even though the story is still unfolding, the aviation emissions case warrants careful analysis for light it sheds on the context and conditions of the EU's role as a global actor and influential regulator in climate change.

Second, this contribution suggests that the EU has moved beyond its diplomatic and rhetorical strategy of invoking its normative leadership example towards what we might interpret as *coercion with kid gloves*. The EU imposed its aviation emissions rule unilaterally and extra-territorially, but then backed off once the international community took action that holds the promise of emulating the EU approach to mitigating aviation's impact on climate change. The EU's action in effect transformed the negotiating context from bargaining without the prospect of exclusion from the EU's market to one in which bargaining took place against the backdrop of a credible threat that the EU would impose costs on flights to and from its territory.

Third, the analysis challenges the scholarly debates that pit conceptions of 'normative power Europe' (NPE) against those of 'market power Europe' (MPE). NPE approaches typically characterize the EU as a unique actor in world affairs whose identity and power are premised on the 'promotion of norms in a normative way', i.e., preference for multilateralism, respect for international law, and use of non-coercive means to exert influence, etc. (Manners

2002).[1] In contrast, MPE emphasizes the EU's 'material existence' and its core identity as the world's largest single market, supplying it with powerful economic resources including the ability to influence international affairs (Damro 2012). The aviation emissions case problematizes such 'either/or' characterizations of the EU, illustrating instead how the EU pursues normative ends (reducing climate change) through unilateral and extraterritorial means, not just persuasion and directional leadership. This contribution thus highlights the false dichotomy between normative power Europe and market power Europe.

The rest of the contribution is organized in five parts. It begins by situating the aviation emissions case within the broader context of the EU's role as a global environmental leader, especially in combatting climate change through its cornerstone policy instrument – the Emissions Trading System (ETS). A brief consideration of the Copenhagen failure illustrates the need to carefully distinguish advocacy from influence and reveals the limits of persuasion in global climate change politics. Next, the case study is set up by spelling out what ICAO did (or did not do) to address greenhouse gas emissions from aviation, how it takes decisions and the EU's uncomfortable place within this UN specialized agency.

The main part of the contribution then provides a narrative account of the case from the specificities of the aviation directive to its temporary suspension, with a focus on how the EU's action prompted the issue to be taken up seriously by ICAO. In doing so, it makes the case that the EU's move to include aviation in its ETS was the decisive factor. The contribution then advances the argument that the EU has intentionally exploited the coercive impact of its decision, but has done so primarily through the credible threat of imposition rather than imposition itself. Before concluding, the contribution revisits the NPE versus MPE dichotomy to consider what light the aviation case sheds on the debate. The conclusion summarizes the three arguments, highlighting which of the EU's regulatory attributes were most salient in getting the outcome it wanted, and closes with a comment on how the empirics of the case shed theoretical light on nature of the EU's power and source of its influence in global environmental politics.

THE EU AS A GLOBAL LEADER ON CLIMATE CHANGE: THE LIMITS OF PERSUASION

European leadership in global environmental governance emerged with the 1992 UN Conference on the Environment and Development where climate change was first seriously addressed in a multilateral forum. Both the EU and its member states were signatory parties to the resulting treaty, the United Nations Framework Convention on Climate Change (UNFCC), that entered into force in 1994, and the subsequent Kyoto Protocol, which was adopted in 1997. It is worth noting that the preceding decade had seen the emergence of environmental movements and electoral successes of green parties across Europe and treaty changes at the EU level that shifted decision-making on

THE EUROPEAN UNION AS A GLOBAL REGULATOR?

environmental matters from unanimity to qualified majority voting, which enabled harmonization of environmental standards at high levels of protection regionally and the promotion of these stricter standards internationally (Jupille and Caporaso 1998; Kelemen 2011; Sbragia and Damro 1999). As a result, the EU's regulatory capacity and the stringency of its rules concerning climate change increased, particularly with the 2003 adoption of the Emissions Trading Systems (ETS) Directive.[2] The ETS was the first – and remains by far the biggest – international system for trading greenhouse gas emission allowances. The ETS works by putting a price on carbon, giving a monetary value to each ton of emissions saved, thereby incentivizing investment in clean technologies and low-carbon solutions. This mandatory 'cap and trade' mechanism covers approximately 50 per cent of the EU's greenhouse gas emissions.

In addition to the ambitious emissions trading scheme and the early and positive role played by the EU on climate change, two other factors have contributed to the widespread perception of the EU as a global environmental leader. First is the tendency in the scholarly literature to conflate the EU's aspirational goals and declarations of leadership with actual results or influence on other actors, as well as the failure to clearly distinguish motivations from outcomes (Damro 2012; Kelemen 2011; Manners 2002). Second, when leadership claims are asserted about the EU's role in global environmental governance, it is often done by comparison with the United States, which has been reticent on climate change to say the least (at least until 2014), which makes the EU look good by comparison (Bomberg 2009; Bretherton and Vogler 2006).

The negotiations leading to the Kyoto Protocol sought to agree specific targets for reductions in emissions of CO_2 and other greenhouse gases emitted by industrialized countries. The EU was the persistent international frontrunner, favouring 15 per cent reductions (from 1990 levels), whereas the United States, even under President Clinton, preferred less-ambitious goals, objected to countries such as China and India being exempt and then eventually (under the Bush administration) pulled out of the agreement altogether in 2001. Despite the EU's inability to secure US participation in the Kyoto agreement, one scholar maintained that:

> EU leadership on Kyoto should be viewed as a relatively successful case of managing globalization. Kyoto has 178 signatories, and the EU has played a pivotal role in persuading key hold-out states such as Russia to participate. Moreover, the EU has been able to use the framework provided by Kyoto and the UN Framework Convention on Climate Change (UNFCC) – with tools such as 'Clean Development Mechanism' (CDM) – projects to encourage developing countries to join the effort to combat climate change and to encourage them to adopt EU standards and technologies when doing so. (Kelemen 2011: 46)

The operative words here are 'persuade' and 'encourage' and are emblematic of the prevailing mode of behaviour or bargaining strategy for the EU in climate change negotiations up until it made the provocative decision to include aviation emissions in the ETS.

Several factors contributed to the growing assertiveness of the EU in climate change politics. It had achieved even greater integration throughout the 2000s. It increased in size from 15 to 27 (now 28) member states. It strengthened its own climate policies, such as adopting the 20-20-20 targets in 2008 and enacting the climate and energy package of 2009. The 20-20-20 targets aspired to by 2020 are: to reduce EU greenhouse gas emissions by 20 per cent from 1990 levels; to improve energy efficiency by 20 per cent; and to raise the share of EU consumption produced from renewable resources to 20 per cent. The EU also increased institutional and legal capacity to be a more coherent and effective international actor. The Lisbon Treaty, which entered into force just before the Copenhagen summit, reaffirmed the EU's commitment to regional and worldwide environmental protection and introduced a specific reference to the goal of combating climate change. The Treaty also asserts the EU's leading role on the world stage in this area and reflects the prominent place climate change has gained on the EU's environmental and energy agenda.

The EU's failure to influence the outcome at Copenhagen was all the more significant because of the meeting's declared goal of producing a successor treaty to the Kyoto Protocol combined with the EU's ambitious, self-assumed leadership role in getting such an agreement. The EU offered to decrease its emissions by 20 to 30 per cent below 1990 levels by 2020 and by 80 to 95 per cent by 2050. The more ambitious proposal of 30 per cent reduction by 2020 was contingent upon other developed countries committing to comparable goals and the developing countries contributing according to their capabilities. Yet, Copenhagen concluded with no takers for the EU's proposals for binding emissions reductions, which highlighted the EU's stark lack of influence, as widely noted by the global media.[3] Some scholars have suggested that climate change had become 'part of a broader zero-sum game of status and influence in world politics in which soft/normative-power resources such as EU domestic action on climate change lost relative weight' (Oberthür 2013: 55; Falkner *et al.* 2010). As Groen and Niemann put it:

> The EU's goals seem to have been too ambitious to be reconcilable with the interests of the United States and the BASIC [Brazil, South Africa, India and China] countries. The latter could not be convinced by the normative arguments of the EU to shift their positions. (2012: 315)

Interestingly, the spokesman for the European Commission delegation in Washington DC at the time explicitly asserted that Copenhagen was about the 'Europe [t]rying to lead by example'.[4] However, this strategy proved inadequate for getting the vital buy-in and co-operation of the biggest emitters and progress in moving towards a post-Kyoto regime. Copenhagen thus illustrated the dissonance between the kind of actor the EU is and the good example it offers versus its ability to actually influence other actors. The salient point is that the EU went in with strong proposals that essentially got

THE EUROPEAN UNION AS A GLOBAL REGULATOR?

no traction. Thus, the Copenhagen episode underscores the limits of aspirational or directional leadership.

The EU's success in getting aviation emissions on ICAO's agenda therefore stands out by contrast. Before examining how the EU was able to exert such influence, it is important to understand the origins and nature of ICAO, its role in climate change policy and the EU's difficult status within it.

AVIATION IN THE INTERNATIONAL REGULATORY CONTEXT

Aviation is a global sector *par excellence*, and although commercial air transportation is a service industry that is highly nationalistic, much of its activity takes place cross-nationally with growth in international markets far outpacing expansion in domestic markets. Global aviation has grown significantly, with traffic increasing at an average rate of 4.4 per cent per year during the 1989–2009 period. As a result, although aviation emissions are the source of only 2 to 3 per cent of global greenhouse gases, they are expected to grow around 3–4 per cent per year and are projected to be 70 per cent higher in 2020 than in 2005, even if fuel efficiency improves by 2 per cent per year (Staniland 2012). Direct emissions from aviation account for about 3 per cent of the EU's total greenhouse gas emissions, the large majority of which comes from international flights, and overall the EU is responsible for about one-third of global aviation emissions.[5]

As the case study will show, the EU had been grappling with this important and growing source of greenhouse gas emissions for some time, and it had specifically (and repeatedly) requested that ICAO take the issue up as it had been mandated to do through the Kyoto Protocol. In fact, as early as the late 1990s the EU set an initial deadline for ICAO action and extended it several times.[6] Arguably the failure of ICAO to act spurred the EU's decision to pursue its own measures.

The international regulatory regime for aviation was set up in 1944 with the signing of the Chicago Convention, which enshrined the principle of state sovereignty as the cornerstone of the international system and established a UN specialized agency, the International Civil Aviation Organization (ICAO), a multilateral body within which decisions governing industry standards are adopted (Kassim 2014). ICAO has two key bodies: an Assembly comprised of all the member states (currently 191), which meets once every three years to provide general policy guidelines and take decisions; and the Council, a permanent body comprised of 36 members elected by the Assembly that governs in the interim. Council membership is constituted with regard to three broad categories: (1) states of chief importance in air transport; (2) states making the largest contribution to provision of facilities for international civil air navigation; and (3) states ensuring geographic representation.[7] In addition to passing resolutions and recommendations, the ICAO Assembly adopts legally binding standards and recommends practices that are included in the annexes to the ICAO Convention.

49

As Staniland (2012: 1011) emphasizes, ICAO's creation came long before aviation was associated with any form of environmental damage and 'its intent was exclusively to create an equitable trading regime for aviation'. Even though environmental protection is not among the explicit objectives of the ICAO, the Convention allowed for the creation of committees as appropriate and the Assembly did in fact set up the Committee on Aviation Environmental Protection (CAEP) as early as 1983 to address noise pollution as well as aircraft engine emissions (Oberthür and Gehring 2006). Furthermore, within the larger UN framework, Article 2.2 of the Kyoto Protocol mandated a core role for ICAO in greenhouse gas emissions reductions for industrialized countries. This explicit institutional remit for action against the backdrop of dramatic changes within the international aviation sector and the evolving international climate regime are what make the relative inaction from ICAO, at least in the eyes of the EU, indefensible.

Yet, the EU's status within ICAO makes its potential influence all the more challenging. The EU member states, not the Union, have legal representation and formal membership. The EU is only an observer, but since 2005 it has had a permanent representative based at the ICAO headquarters in Montreal. The EU's representative attends ICAO meetings, briefs EU member states representatives and works to strengthen their unity and co-operation, as well as informs members of the ICAO Council of EU policy and generally ensures that the EU's positions are well known (Kassim 2014; Staniland 2012). As reflected in the discourses of many its members and statements by the ICAO secretariat, the EU's status is characterized as 'anomalous' i.e., it is clearly more active than most regional organizations, but it does not enjoy the voting and speaking privileges of members (Kassim and Stevens 2010: 159; Dabrowksi 2014: 138).

THE INCLUSION OF AVIATION IN THE ETS: THE EU CHALLENGE TO ICAO

One crucial element in empirically establishing the EU's pivotal role in getting action on aviation emissions on ICAO's agenda is the question of timing. The EU had been agitating about the issue for over a decade, ever since it first responded to the 1999 study published by Intergovernmental Panel on Climate Change (IPCC) highlighting the atmospheric impact of air transport. Subsequent to this influential study and the EU's adoption of the Kyoto Protocol, the Emissions Trading System (ETS) Directive was passed in 2003 and remains the core policy instrument in the EU's approach to combatting climate change.

Although action on aviation was considered initially, emissions from aviation were not included in the original ETS Directive. The explanation for this was chiefly that there were ongoing environmental impact studies by the Commission, divisions among some member states and varying positions within the

THE EUROPEAN UNION AS A GLOBAL REGULATOR?

industry itself (Staniland 2012). There was also an assumption that ICAO would take action as mandated by the Kyoto Protocol.

Even though aviation was not included in the emissions trading scheme, the issue was far from dead. In 2005, the member states charged the Commission with preparing a Green Paper to design a comprehensive general strategy for achieving 'sustainable, competitive, and secure energy'.[8] By October 2006, the Commission presented detailed proposals for reforming the ETS to address problems such as surplus carbon allowances and to include aviation in the second phase of the emissions trading scheme. The legislation, which broadly amended the original ETS Directive, was adopted in December 2008 and took effect on 2 February 2009.[9]

The directive specified that commercial aviation should be subject to the ETS by January 2012, although for reasons associated with the complexity of compliance and the need to register aircraft in the system, some preliminary measures did go into effect by 2009. The inclusion of aviation in the ETS envisioned limiting emissions to 95 per cent of the levels of the average annual emissions of the 2004–2006 period. Each airline was initially to receive 85 per cent of its allocation of carbon allowances for free (Directive 2008/101, Article 1, 3s and Article 3d).

Most significant was the decision to apply the scheme not just to flights within and between countries participating in the ETS, but to the entirety of all international flights landing in or departing from EU airports. The decision to apply the ETS to emissions from the entirety of the route, rather than to just the portion in EU airspace represented a dramatic externalization of its policy. The Commission defended this approach as the best way to reap the maximum environmental benefits and to further protect the global commons (Staniland 2012:1012–14). While the ETS has had its fair share of criticisms as well as challenges to its effective implementation, it was not until the EU made the move to extend the scheme to include emissions from international aviation, that it confronted a legal or jurisdictional challenge.

EU–ICAO Interactions

As Staniland (2012) depicted it, ICAO and the EU had essentially been at a stand-off over the controversial extension of the ETS to non-European airlines since the Assembly meeting in 2007. At that Assembly, ICAO's members, despite the opposition of a European bloc comprising nearly '20% of ICAO's membership' (27 EU member states, plus 15 other European states)[10] had adopted a resolution (A36-22; Appendix L), which (among other things), 'Urge[d] Contracting States not to implement an emissions trading system on other Contracting States' aircraft operators except on the basis of mutual agreement between those States.' That was precisely what the EU was planning to do as their aviation emissions directive and extension to international flights was set to go into effect in January of 2012.

The EU's plans to address aviation emissions unilaterally, however, did produce some changes within ICAO. The 2007 Assembly did request that the Council:

> form a new Group on International Aviation and Climate Change composed of senior government officials representative of all ICAO regions, with the equitable participation of developing and developed countries ... for the purpose of developing and recommending to the Council an aggressive Programme of Action on International Aviation and Climate Change, based on consensus, and reflecting the shared vision and strong will of all Contracting States. (Appendix K).

Prior to establishing the Group on International Aviation and Climate Change (GIACC), discussion of aviation emissions in ICAO had taken place in its Committee on Aviation Environmental Protection (CAEP), but these discussions had focused on the technical aspects of including aviation emissions in domestic emissions trading schemes (International Civil Aviation Organization [ICAO] 2007: 80–3). Divisions among the members, however, were such that the GIACC could not reach a consensus on addressing aviation emissions, beyond the desirability of improving fuel efficiency, and it was wound up in June 2009 (GIACC 2009).[11] The High-level Meeting on International Aviation and Climate Change (HLM-ENV/09), which was set up to review the recommendations of GIACC, in October 2009 declared that 'ICAO will establish a process to develop a framework for market based measures in international aviation.' The EU's 2006 decision to include aviation in the ETS, therefore, had clearly prompted discussion and incremental movement.

There was further movement at 37th Assembly of ICAO in 2010, which took forward the recommendation of the High-level Meeting. Resolution A37-19 included several steps on climate change:

- set a medium-term global aspirational goal of keeping the global net carbon emissions from international aviation from 2020 at the same level;
- '*encouraged*' states to submit their action plans outlining their respective policies and actions, and annual reporting on international aviation CO_2 emissions to ICAO, although it accepted that states whose international aviation activity falls below 1 per cent of total revenue ton kilometres would not have to submit action plans (a *de minimus* clause); and
- 'requested' that the Council develop a framework for market-based measures (MBMs) in international aviation for consideration by the 2013 Assembly.

Although the resolution did not contain specific targets and the language remains largely 'aspirational', the persistent pressure from the EU clearly had some influence in that it is the first time ICAO members expressed support for a 'cap-and-trade' approach to mitigate international aviation emissions. Furthermore, as Staniland's (2012) analysis illustrated, the EU was successful in getting a majority backing to block a US-proposed requirement that there must be 'mutual agreement' by states to their inclusion in emissions schemes created by others. In fact, because of this achievement, the EU hereafter begins to show more conciliatory gestures, including raising the possibility of excluding from ETS liability all flights arriving at EU airports from non-EU states and applying it only to outgoing flights. Many critics suggested that this concession was a step too far, while supporters argued that this gesture was contingent on non-EU states adopting measures equivalent to the ETS. Staniland concluded that these developments in fact showed the EU's its determination 'not to deviate from the ETS legislation' (2012: 1017).

The next major development occurred after the ICAO's Council meeting held in 2012 where the 36 members agreed on the establishment of yet another a High-level Group on International Aviation and Climate Change 'to develop recommendations on a series of policy issues related to international aviation and climate change, including those related to MBMs, and to report on progress concerning a proposal for the 2013 Assembly Resolution' [12] Sufficiently pleased with the progress in the Council to deliver on the 2010 Assembly's charge to develop a proposal for an ICAO resolution, the European Commission then announced that it would suspend the requirement that non-EU airlines surrender emission allowances for flights into and out of Europe under the ETS.[13] The Commission made clear, however, that if the forthcoming 38th Assembly meeting in 2013 did 'not deliver', then international aviation emissions would automatically be included in the ETS.[14]

When the 2013 ICAO Assembly adopted the resolution agreeing to deliver a global plan to curb global aviation emissions by its next meeting in 2016 and to be implemented in 2020, the Commission formally agreed to suspend the application of EU Directive 2008/101 to flights between the EU and European Economic Area and other countries for one year. The Commission's so-called 'Stop the Clock' initiative was only a temporary derogation, however. In the absence of a subsequent permanent amendment of the aviation ETS, the scheme would automatically revert to its original full scope. In April 2014, the European Parliament and the Council of the European Union adopted a regulation amending the 2008 directive such that non- EU carriers would be exempt from the aviation emissions trading scheme. The new legislation states that the objective is to 'introduce a temporary derogation for the monitoring, reporting and surrendering of allowances from flights to and from countries outside the EEA from 1 January 2013 to 31 December 2016'.[15] Clause 5 of the Regulation clarifies that:

> The derogations provided for in this Regulation take into account the results of bilateral and multilateral contacts with third countries, which the Commission will continue to pursue on behalf of the Union, in order to promote the use of market-based mechanisms to reduce emissions from aviation.[16]

The coincidence of timing thus suggests that the EU's extension of the ETS to the entirety of all flights to and from the EU can be seen as the critical factor that prompted ICAO's members into action. Given the temporary suspension, it continues to serve as a stick in this complex interaction between the EU and

ICAO's other members. Despite years of prodding, there was no effective action on aviation emissions in ICAO until the EU made its move to include aviation in its ETS and threatened to apply it to all international flights.

ALTERNATIVE EXPLANATIONS

There are two potential alternative explanations for why ICAO finally put the aviation emissions issue on its agenda in a serious way. One, consistent with the general literature on the EU's role in climate change and normative power, is that EU's directional leadership or persuasion did eventually work and effectively changed the preferences of its opponents, thereby getting support needed within ICAO. The other possible explanation is that the airline industry and its pressure on ICAO members provided the real source of influence in this case. A brief examination of the reactions of other states and the role of the International Air Transport Association, however, shows that the EU's unilateral decision to apply its ETS to aviation extraterritorially was clearly the driving force behind the ICAO's action.

First, there is no indication that other ICAO members changed their positions. Both before and subsequent to its adoption, ICAO members attacked the EU's emissions regime for aviation on legal and economic grounds. The non-EU members of ICAO claimed that the EU action violated the Chicago Convention by imposing an illegal charge based on liability for emissions on their airlines whenever they fly to or from EU airports. Opponents also charged that the EU's creation of a regional scheme for aviation emissions usurped the mandate given to ICAO under the Kyoto Protocol (Oberthur 2013; Staniland 2012). Though many countries, including India, Russia and even Canada, joined in the chorus of complaints about the EU's move to impose its emissions scheme unilaterally, the discussion here will focus on China and the United States as the two most consequential bilateral interactions, given their economic size and strategic relationships with the EU.

China's reaction was primarily an economic one, essentially threatening a trade war. Although there were many countries opposed to the EU's unilateral move and both the BASIC nations and another group of 20 countries convened in Moscow in early 2012 submitted formal written complaints to ICAO, the Chinese government stood out in the vigour of its opposition. As early as 2011 it issued a directive to their airlines prohibiting them from participating in the EU-ETS. It also froze an order to purchase Airbus A330 aircraft worth an estimated $6 billion.[17] This shows quite clearly that China was not persuaded by the EU's example and in fact was willing to fight it with retaliatory trade measures.

The United States took a decidedly more legal approach, but one that is equally forceful in showing that the EU was not successful in its leadership by example strategy. The US House of Representatives passed a bill allowing US airlines to 'disregard' the EU law obliging them to buy carbon permits when flying into and out of Europe. Though the predicted cost to the airline

THE EUROPEAN UNION AS A GLOBAL REGULATOR?

industry was certainly a motivation for the action, the rationale for the bill was put into broader terms:

> This appropriately named EU scheme is an arbitrary and unjust violation of international law that disadvantages US air carriers, threatens US aviation jobs, and could close down direct travel from many central and western US airports to Europe.[18]

The US Senate also passed a similar bill, and President Obama signed what became Public Law 112-200 on 27 November 2012. The 'European Union Emissions Trading Scheme Prohibition Act of 2011' as explicitly conveyed in the name of the Act, prohibited US operators of civil aircraft from participating in the EU's aviation ETS. Further illustrating the strong opposition and the view that the EU infringed international law and the integrity of the Chicago System, US Transportation Secretary, in testimony before the Senate, referred to the EU's ETS aviation measures as 'lone-ranger' unilateralism and a lousy policy.[19] These reactions clearly indicate that the US, like China, did not change its position.

What about the role of the airlines and the degree of influence they may have exerted over ICAO? The US airline industry – through the Air Transport Association (ATA) – unsuccessfully challenged the EU's policy before the European Court of Justice, indicating that it was not quick to change its position. In the run-up to the 2010 ICAO Assembly meeting, however, the International Air Transport Association (IATA), representing the interests of the airline industries, moved precipitously towards favouring a global cap-and-trade system and vowed to prod the IACO Assembly along to pass a resolution on the development of a global framework on market-based measures.[20] Yet, despite the strong industry support (which was much in line with the EU position), the story was still much the same, as a push for an international framework for aviation emissions reduction using a market-based approach could not overcome 'reservations expressed by some States over the implementation' of these measures (International Civil Aviation Organization [ICAO] 2011: 31). Thus, the change in positions in ICAO did not coincide with a change in the positions of the airlines, but followed the EU's extension of the ETS to aviation. This interpretation is borne out by industry and state actors, who give the EU at least partial credit for ICAO agreeing to tackle the aviation emissions. Following the 2013 ICAO decision, IATA Director General Tony Tyler commented that the EU role was decisive:

> The EU ETS, whilst it created tensions between States, also prompted action at a global level, and their willingness to 'stop the clock' on extra-European flights provided the necessary welcome relief of tension in the discussions. Aviation would not be in the climate leadership position it is in today were it not for the early and persistent effort of the European Commission and Parliament, which inspired both industry and other governments.[21]

THE EUROPEAN UNION AS A GLOBAL REGULATOR?

Further support for the argument that the ICAO decision cannot be significantly attributed to industry pressure is the comment from the United Kingdom (UK) Sustainable Aviation Council:

> Whatever emerges from the next ICAO assembly, the EU gets at least some recognition for compelling the UN body to act ... The EU got ICAO to take emissions seriously and deserves credit; At least people are talking about it, which wasn't the case in the past.[22]

Ultimately, the EU's role was indisputably pivotal even if it remains to be seen whether ICAO and its members will follow through in a satisfactory way for the 2016 Assembly.

COERCION WITH KID GLOVES? FROM EU UNILATERALISM TOWARDS A GLOBAL APPROACH

The preceding discussion clearly illustrates that the EU's inclusion of emissions from the entirety of flights to and from the EU imposed costs on non-EU airlines and that their positions and those of their home governments subsequently changed. The aviation emissions case illustrates that the size of the EU's market, the stringency of its rules and its regulatory capacity enabled it to shape ICAO's agenda. More specifically, the extension of the ETS to include emissions from aviation marked a shift from bargaining without exclusion to bargaining with exclusion, and, as specified in the framework article (Young 2015), this becomes the critical explanatory variable in this case.

Because the EU's regulatory move to include the entirety of flights to and from the EU in the ETS imposed costs on non-EU firms, the coercive effect of its decision are clear. What is less clear is whether that was its intention. The existing literature is divided. Staniland (2012) emphasizes that the inclusion of the entire flight in the ETS was motivated by ensuring the effectiveness of the policy in reducing greenhouse gas emissions. Scott and Rajamani (2013), by contrast, refer to the EU's decision to extend its ETS to the aviation sector as 'contingent unilateralism' or 'multilateralism forcing' – deploying unilateral policies only reluctantly and with a goal of incentivizing regulatory action elsewhere. Scott (2014: 97) also characterizes this case as an example of the EU seeking 'to galvanize third country or global action to tackle transboundary problems and to pursue objectives that have been internationally agreed upon'.

Whether the intention was to prompt international action, the Commission certainly seems to have embraced the coercive potential of the policy to do so. Then European Commissioner for Climate Action Connie Hedegaard's explanation of the Commission's willingness to suspend the extension of the ETS to aviation pending action by ICAO claimed that the EU: 'firmly desires an international framework tackling carbon dioxide emissions from aviation, and the proposal to defer has been made since many countries are now prepared to take action within ICAO and even prepared to move toward a global market-based mechanism'. She went on, however, 'if this exercise does not deliver

THE EUROPEAN UNION AS A GLOBAL REGULATOR?

– and I hope it does – then needless to say we are [automatically] back to where we are today with the EU ETS.'[23] The EU, therefore, is using the credible threat of imposing costs on non-EU airlines, rather than the imposition of costs itself to encourage international co-operation that it desires. This stance might best be characterized as 'coercion with kid gloves' and reinforces the argument made here that the EU used its coercive capacity, essentially its market power, to influence the behaviour of other actors even beyond its own airspace, and it did so to pursue its normative agenda of addressing aviation's contribution to climate change as vigorously as possible.

THE LIMITS OF THE NORMATIVE POWER/MARKET POWER DICHOTOMY

The EU's relatively gentle exploitation of the coercive effect of its unilateral policy to pursue the objective of multilateral action to address climate change illustrates well that neither normative example nor market power considered in isolation, as suggested by the conceptualizations of normative or market power Europe, provides a compelling explanation of the EU's success or failure in shaping global affairs. The problem arising from scholarly debates about the comparative utility of normative versus market power Europe approaches is precisely that they tend to over-emphasize the singularity of either ideational or material factors as representations of the EU's identity or power, rather than reflecting the dynamic character of EU policymaking and action in the world. For theoretical or analytical purposes, such characterizations lock the EU into a static frame rather than acknowledging the ambiguity and open-ended, dynamic, and sometimes contradictory, characteristics of a complex polity such as the EU. The original articulations of both MPE and NPE are more nuanced than this, and the aviation emissions case serves to underscore the original intuitions and insights of both Damro and Manners. Damro claims that the point of MPE is not:

> to inspire analytical intolerance of norms-based and other approaches, but rather to encourage new avenues of research into the EU as a power and the possible compatibility of other conceptualizations with market power insights. For example, in which ways do normative justifications interact with material incentives? (Damro 2012: 697)

Manners, on the other hand, argues that 'we must judge the EU's creative efforts to promote a more just, cosmopolitical world in terms of its principles, actions and impact' (Manners 2008: 47). The point here is that both authors and the respective approaches they advocate contain significant insights and analytical injunctions for the other, and the aviation case helps bring forth these general compatibilities rather than continuing to position them as analytical oppositions or, worse, false dichotomies.

Further, as the aviation emissions case suggests, the normative and market power conceptualizations and explanatory claims could benefit from the empirical goals laid out by the analytical framework of this collection, particularly the attempt to specify how the EU's attributes and its structural exploitation of them matter, under what conditions and in which contexts. In the case of aviation greenhouse gas emissions the EU is certainly pursuing a value (climate change mitigation), but is doing so in a way that is unilateral, runs contrary to the established norm of state sovereignty, and is coercive. Thus, the ends, but not the means, are consistent with the expectations of behaviour from the normative power Europe conceptualization. The converse, however, holds as well. The market power Europe conceptualization stresses how the EU exercises influence, but not to what end.

The rationale for including aviation in ETS was motivated by environmental considerations and the design of the system was more in keeping with that objective than the concern for competitive disadvantages, as limiting to European airspace would have been sufficient for that end. Although certainly European airlines were concerned about market distortions and unfair financial burdens, they did not pressure the Commission to abandon the aviation emissions scheme altogether, but rather continued to express their support for a global approach. Interestingly, the industry perspective also couched their position in environmental impact terms as well. For instance, Athar Husain Khan, acting Secretary General of the Association of European Airlines (AEA) commented in reaction to the 'Stop the Clock' measure:

> European airlines will still be required to buy ETS credits for their flights within the EU. Since these are such a tiny proportion of worldwide CO2, it shows the inability of a purely regional scheme to have meaningful impact on what is a global issue.[24]

Additionally, the industry view has been, generally speaking, more closely aligned with the European Parliament's perspective than that of the Council or certain member states with regard to greater environmental stringency and various other issues related to the wider ETS reform debates.

CONCLUSION

The European Commission and many others hailed ICAO's 2013 resolution to develop by 2016 a global MBM to address aviation emissions to start in 2020 as a landmark decision and historic breakthrough after the inertia over the past decade or so. Indeed, if the ICAO high-level working group delivers the promised framework in 2016, the aviation industry is set to become the first international transport sector to apply a global market-based mechanism to reduce their emissions, and the evidence here suggests this would likely not have occurred in the absence of the EU's challenge to it authority by devising its own approach to be applied internationally. The contribution has demonstrated that the EU's decision to incorporate aviation into its emissions trading scheme played a pivotal role in getting the issue on ICAO's agenda. Thus, the critical explanatory variable in this case of EU influence was the shift in the EU's

THE EUROPEAN UNION AS A GLOBAL REGULATOR?

strategy of bargaining without exclusion to bargaining with the threat of exclusion. This conclusion is supported by the coincidence in timing between EU policy developments and international reactions and by the assessments of industry representatives and government officials.

While the coercive effect of the EU's actions are clear, this contribution has not sought to answer whether that was the intent behind the decision to include the entirety of flights to and from the EU in its Emissions Trading Scheme. What is clear, however, is that the EU has sought to exploit that coercive impact, even if it has done so primarily through the credible threat of imposing costs rather than the actual imposition of those costs, having temporarily suspended the application of the ETS to aviation. Consequently, this analysis has illustrated the shortcomings of explanations of EU international action that are too closely wedded to conceptualizations of the EU as either a normative or market power. In this case, the EU has pursued the normative end of multilateral action to address climate change through the unilateral imposition of a policy that challenges state sovereignty and which coercively leverages the significance of the EU's large market. These limitations in the scholarly literature illustrate the need for more rigorous frameworks like the one attempted in this collection to push knowledge of EU influence beyond interpretation towards systematic explanation.

Biographical note: Vicki L. Birchfield is associate professor in the Sam Nunn School of International Affairs at the Georgia Institute of Technology.

ACKNOWLEDGMENTS

I wish to thank the two anonymous reviewers for valuable comments on this manuscript. Appreciation also goes to Andrew Wirt for his research assistance, and I am especially grateful to the guest editor of this collection, Alasdair Young, for his helpful and generous guidance.

NOTES

1 For further discussion of the critiques, extensions and refinements of the NPE approach see Whitman (2011) and Birchfield (2013).
2 Directive 2003/87/EC of the European Parliament and the Council of Ministers, 13 October 2003, setting up 'a scheme for greenhouse gas emission trading within the Community'.
3 For examples of criticism of the EU in the press, see, for example: BBC News, 22 December 2009, 'Europe Snubbed in Copenhagen' available at http://www.bbc.co.uk/blogs/legacy/thereporters/gavinhewitt/2009/12/s_5.html and *The New York Times*, 15 January 2010, 'EU Seeks to Regain Influence on Response to Climate Change', available at http://www.nytimes.com/2010/01/16/business/global/16iht-inside16.html (accessed 21 April 2014). For extensive scholarly analysis of this

THE EUROPEAN UNION AS A GLOBAL REGULATOR?

failure to exercise leadership at the Copenhagen summit, see Oberthür (2013) and Groen and Niemann (2012).

4 *ClimateWire: Friday, January 15, 2010*, available at http://www.eenews.net/stories/86478 (accessed 10 October 2014).

5 http://ec.europa.eu/clima/policies/ets/index_en.htm (accessed 9 August 2014).

6 The author acknowledges one of the anonymous reviewers for this insight.

7 http://www.icao.int/about-icao/Pages/council.aspx (accessed 21 April 2014).

8 http://eur-lex.europa.eu/legal-content/EN/TXT/?uri=CELEX:52006DC0105 (accessed 23 April 2014).

9 Directive 2008/101/EC of the European Parliament and of the Council of 19 November 2008 amending Directive 2003/87/EC so as to include aviation activities in the scheme for greenhouse gas emission allowance trading within the Community, [2009] OJ, L 8/3 [Directive 2008/101].

10 Annual Report of the Council, ICAO 2007, 39–43. http://www.icao.int/environmental-protection/Documents/Env_Report_07.pdf (accessed 13 January 2015).

11 http://www.icao.int/environmental-protection/Pages/group-international-aviation-climate-change.aspx (accessed 23 April 2015).

12 ICAO, ICAO News Release, COM 20/12, 'New ICAO Council High-level Group to Focus on Environmental Policy Challenges' (15 November 2012) available at http://www.icao.int/Newsroom/Pages/new-ICAO-council-high-level-group-to-focus-on-environmental-policy-challenges.aspx (accessed 23 April 2015).

13 http://ec.europa.eu/clima/news/articles/news_2012111202_en.htm (accessed 23 April 2015).

14 http://europa.eu/rapid/press-release_MEMO-12-854_en.htm (accessed 23 April 2015).

15 Regulation (EU) No 421/2014 of the European Parliament and of the Council of 16 April 2014 amending Directive 2003/87/EC establishing a scheme for greenhouse gas emission allowance trading within the Community, in view of the implementation by 2020 of an international agreement applying a single global market-based measure to international aviation emissions. http://eur-lex.europa.eu/legal-content/EN/TXT/?uri=CELEX:32014R0421 (accessed 21 April 2015).

16 Regulation (EU) No 421/2014 of the European Parliament and of the Council of 16 April 2014 amending Directive 2003/87/EC establishing a scheme for greenhouse gas emission allowance trading within the Community, in view of the implementation by 2020 of an international agreement applying a single global market-based measure to international aviation emissions. http://eur-lex.europa.eu/legal-content/EN/TXT/?uri=CELEX:32014R0421 (accessed 21 April 2015).

17 http://www.euractiv.com/sections/transport/chinas-trade-war-threats-over-aviation-emissions-not-serious-meps-say-301263 (accessed 16 April 2014).

18 http://www.aircargoworld.com/Air-Cargo-News/2011/10/u-s-house-votes-to-ban-eu-ets-participation/262794 (accessed 20 April 2014.

19 http://www.greenaironline.com/news.php?viewStory=1505 (accessed 20 August 2014).

20 For evidence of IATA's commitment and early efforts to influence ICAO and its members, see http://www.iata.org/pressroom/pr/Pages/2009-12-08-01.aspx (accessed 13 January 2015); see also Staniland (2012: 1016).

21 http://www.greenaironline.com/news.php?viewStory=1763 (accessed 28 August 2014).

22 http://www.euractiv.com/sections/aviation/icao-under-pressure-forge-deal-aviation-emissions-303563 (accessed 1 September 2014).

23 European Commission (EC), News, 'Commission proposes to "stop the clock" on international aviation in the EU ETS pending 2013 ICAO General Assembly' (12

THE EUROPEAN UNION AS A GLOBAL REGULATOR?

November 2012), Newsroom, Climate Action, European Commission, available at http://ec.europa.eu/clima/news/articles/news_2012111202_en.htm (accessed 1 September 2014).

24 http://www.greenaironline.com/news.php?viewStory=1659 (accessed 20 April 2015).

REFERENCES

Birchfield, V. (2013) 'A normative power Europe framework of transnational policy formation', *Journal of European Public Policy* 20(6): 907–22.

Bomberg, E. (2009) 'Governance for sustainable development: the US and EU compared', in M. Schreurs, H. Selin, and S. Van DeVeer (eds), *Transatlantic Environmental and Energy Politics*, fARNHAM: Ashgate, PP. 21–40.

Bretherton, C. and Vogler, J. (2006) *The European Union as a Global Actor*, 2nd ed., London: Routledge.

Damro, C. (2012) 'Market power Europe', *Journal of European Public Policy* 19(5): 682–99.

Dabrowksi, M. (2014) 'Transport policy: the EU as taker, shaper or shaker of the global civil aviation regime', in G. Falkner and P. Müller (eds), *EU Policies in a Global Perspective: Shaping or Taking International Regimes?* London: Routledge, pp. 130–48.

Falkner, R., Stephan, H. and Vogler, J., (2010) 'International climate policy after Copenhagen: toward a "building blocks" approach', *Global Policy* 1(3): 252–62.

Groen, L. and Niemann, A. (2013) 'The European Union at the Copenhagen climate negotiations: a case of contested EU actorness and effectiveness', *International Relations* 27(3): 308–24.

International Civil Aviation Organization (ICAO) (2007) *ICAO Environmental Report 2007*, Montreal: International Civil Aviation Organizations Publications, available at http://www.icao.int/environmental-protection/Documents/Env_Report_07.pdf.

International Civil Aviation Organization (ICAO) (2011) *Annual Report of the Council 2010*, Montreal: International Civil Aviation Organizations Publications, available at http://www.icao.int/publications/Documents/9952_en.pdf.

Jupille, J. and Caporaso, J. (1998) 'States, agency, and rules: the European Union in global environmental politics', in C. Rhodes (ed.), *The European Union in the World Community*, Boulder, CO: Lynne Rienner, pp. 213–29.

Kassim, H. (2014) 'Re-writing the rules: the impact and limitations of the EU as an actor in international aviation', Paper presented to the International Studies Association Conference, Toronto, 26–29 March 2014.

Kassim, H. and Stevens, H. (2010) *Air Transport and the European Union*, New York: Palgrave Macmillan.

Kelemen, R.D. (2011) 'Globalizing European Union environmental policy', in W. Jacoby and S. Meunier (eds), *Europe and the Management of Globalization*, London: Routledge, pp. 37–51.

Manners, I. (2002) 'Normative power Europe: a contradiction in terms?', *Journal of Common Market Studies* 4(2): 235–58.

Oberthür, S. (2013) 'The European Union's performance in the international climate change regime', in S. Oberthür, K.E. Jorgensen and J. Shanin (eds), *The Performance of the EU in International Institution*, London: Routledge, pp. 54–69.

Oberthür, S. and Gehring, T. (eds) (2006) *Institutional Interaction in Global Environmental Governance*, Cambridge, MA: MIT Press.

Sbragia, A. and Damro, C. (1999). 'The changing role of the European Union in international environmental politics', *Environment and Planning C: Government and Policy* 17(1): 53–68.

THE EUROPEAN UNION AS A GLOBAL REGULATOR?

Scott, J. (2014) 'Extraterritoriality and territorial extension in EU law', *The American Journal of Comparative Law* 67: 87–126.

Scott, J. and Rajamani, L. (2013) 'Contingent unilateralism—international aviation in the European Emissions Trading Scheme', in B. Van Vooren, S. Blockmans and J. Wouters (eds), *The EU's Role in Global Governance: The Legal Dimension*, Oxford: Oxford University Press, pp. 209–23.

Staniland, M. (2012) 'Regulating aircraft emissions: leadership and market power', *Journal of European Public Policy* 19(7): 1006–25.

Whitman, R. (ed.) (2011) *Normative Power Europe: Empirical and Theoretical Perspectives*, New York: Palgrave Macmillan.

Young, A.R. (2015) 'The European Union as a global regulator? Context and comparison', *Journal of European Public Policy*, doi: 10.1080/13501763.2015.1046902.

power. Thirdly, there is insufficient variation in the degree of EU influence over regulatory regimes resulting in a failure to identify causal mechanisms and scope conditions. This is a contribution towards addressing these points by examining EU influence over the drafting of the International Labour Organization (ILO) Maritime Labour Convention (MLC) (2006), regarded as the 'fourth pillar' of the global regulatory regime for international shipping alongside the International Maritime Organization's (IMO) International Convention for the Safety of Lives at Sea (SOLAS), International Convention on Standards of Training, Certification and Watchkeeping (STCW), and International Convention for the Prevention of Pollution from Ships (MARPOL). I argue that the EU played a far less important role in the drafting process than the literature on regulation assumes and studies on the MLC have argued. The explanatory variables considered are (1) the failure of EU member states to co-ordinate sufficiently early in the negotiation process; (2) lack of EU cohesion once co-ordinating; (3) the rules-based negotiating environment of the ILO (and its norm of tripartite consensus); and (4) that labour standards are a form of process regulation. While some issues are ILO specific, others travel and contribute to explaining variation in EU regulatory power more generally.

This contribution focuses on the ILO as the principle international organization responsible for global social policy regulation through 'rule-mediated negotiation' (Young 2015: 17). The ILO was founded in 1919 to prevent industrialization and international economic competition forcing working standards downwards in a 'race to the bottom' by setting minimum labour standards that its members ratify and incorporate into national law. It also provides expert legal scrutiny of members' adherence to conventions, a comprehensive complaints procedure and technical assistance to governments unable to implement standards. The ILO has a unique tripartite structure that incorporates trade unionists and employers' groups alongside government officials in the national representation of each ILO member state. Labour standards are drafted in a tripartite manner that seeks consensus whenever possible by giving equal weight to the interests of workers, employers and governments. Consequently, EU member states' voting weight is reduced threefold in comparison to other intergovernmental negotiations. However, when EU interests align with one or both social partners, its influence is increased by combining with their voice in the search for consensus and their votes in a ballot. It is important to note that ILO members are not obliged to ratify conventions and any exertion of regulatory influence through ILO standards is ultimately acquiesced through national government ratification decisions.

By asking to what extent the EU influenced the content of the ILO's MLC, this contribution questions whether and how the EU influences global regulations when it has been actively trying. The literature so far has answered affirmatively, with Tortell *et al.* (2009: 125) stating that 'a cursory analysis of the way in which the convention was adopted and is now being ratified shows that the EU has taken a key position in this process'. I assess the claim that EU was an influential actor in the drafting process of the MLC by examining

THE EUROPEAN UNION AS A GLOBAL REGULATOR?

to what extent the EU shaped five core issues during the entire negotiating process from 2001 to 2006. While the EU undoubtedly became a more coherent actor from 2004 onwards, and successfully influenced a few important issues, this did not amount to significant influence over the core issues of the MLC because most were decided prior to 2004. I show that in three of the issues, the EU had no influence, in the fourth it was limited and in the fifth its major achievement was to insert a regional economic integration organization (REIO) clause. In order to substantiate these claims, process tracing is used to establish how the final regulatory standards agreed in each issue developed during the six-year negotiating period. Attention is paid to (1) when the regulatory standards were agreed; (2) which actors (both EU and non-EU) supported them; (3) the degree of EU coherence during key debates about the standards; and (4) where EU member states stood in the overall spectrum of preferences.

It proceeds in four parts. The first reviews the literature on why the EU might seek to influence ILO standard setting and justifies the case selection. The second develops the variables identified and their connection to the case. The third presents an empirical analysis of ILO documentation of the six years of MLC negotiations and the final section concludes.

THE EU AND REGULATING GLOBAL LABOUR STANDARDS

Empirical studies of EU regulatory influence tend to focus on product or financial standards and how access to the EU market serves as a strong incentive for firms and governments to seek regulatory compliance with EU norms, through adopting the same standards, seeking recognition of equivalence, or bilateral regulation. Economic incentives, the distribution of costs, the degree of interdependence asymmetry, and political power have all been identified as importance explanatory variables determining why, when, how and whose terms regulatory systems converge. But how well do these explanations travel to process regulation such as labour standards? In general, economic competition does not drive process standard conformity in the same way it does for product standards, because excluding non-compliant goods from markets is harder. In turn, this places costs on states with higher standards without imposing penalties on states with lower standards. However, Lazer (2006: 460) argues that 'consistent process standards may lower the costs of multinational corporations (MNCs) that are located in different countries, and as a result, they may put pressure on host countries to adopt compatible rules'. In the MLC negotiations, shipowners' behaved in this way, preferring a widely ratified convention to a limited one, and only giving secondary concern to preferring weaker standards over stronger ones. Politicization is an additional concern to the process regulation of labour standards. When a regulatory authority deems a process non-compliant with a fundamental labour standard, it implies questioning the regulation of private actors within third states. Failure to implement standards places blame on governments, but it is important to differentiate between unwillingness to act as a manifestation of culpability and incapacity to act as a manifestation of weak domestic legal and regulatory institutions. Developing states are wary of labour and environmental regulations being used as a form of protectionism (Orbie and Babarinde 2008), as well as undermining their comparative advantage in the global economy. Since 1998, the ILO has vigorously promoted fundamental labour standards as universal rights, taking a soft-law approach to achieving universal ratification of its eight core labour standards through technical assistance and peer-scrutiny, while also seeking to make ILO standards benchmarks in trade and development agreements (such as the EU's Generalized Scheme of Preferences (GSP+) trade regime for developing countries *cf.* Orbie and Tortell [2009b]).

This contribution investigates the degree of influence the EU had over the drafting of the MLC, an important international legal convention regulating all aspects of employment-related issues on board merchant ships. The shipping industry is one of the most globalized sectors in the world economy, combining multinational workforces aboard ships registered in flag states travelling through international waters to third-state ports. Although the IMO is primarily responsible maritime regulation, since 1920 the ILO has generated 36 conventions, 30 recommendations and one protocol relating to maritime employment, with varying levels of ratification. In 2000, the ILO decided to begin work on an ambitious review of these instruments with the objective of updating and consolidating their content into a single 'super convention' that would serve as a seafarer's 'bill of rights' (ILO 2006a: §13), and constitute the '4th pillar' of international maritime law (ILO 2006a: §28). According to the convention's Preamble, the goal was to 'create a single, coherent instrument embodying as far as possible all up-to-date standards of existing international maritime labour conventions' and that it 'should be designed to secure the widest possible acceptability among governments, shipowners and seafarers', (ILO 2006b: 1–2). The final convention is over 100 pages long and was negotiated over six years according to the ILO's tripartite framework of workers (seafarers), employers (shipowners) and governments, and represents a compromise across the spectrum of interests of ILO members. At the beginning of negotiations, these ranged from forceful advocates of robust social protection to preferences for minimal social standards with greater flexibility in their application. Locating actors on a spectrum of preferences depends on issue area, but generally seafarers sought greater rights, often supported by the Philippines, owing to it being 'the number one maritime labour supplying country' (ILO 2006a: §27). Open register states[1] sat at the opposite end, with the United States (US), Japan and South Korea sharing many of their preferences. Shipowners were disposed to this position, too, but were often willing to compromise for the sake of agreeing a workable convention, locating them more centrally. EU member states' positions varied considerably, ranging from Denmark, Netherlands, Germany and the United Kingdom (UK) advocating high standards, to Malta and Cyprus – two open register states that did not join the EU until 2004 – initially shared preferences with other open register states, although greater coherence was achieved towards the end of negotiations. Despite these differences, a single text was agreed that entered into force on 20 August 2013, '12 months after the date on which there have been registered ratification by at least 30 Members with a total share in the world gross tonnage of ships of at least 33%' (ILO 2006b: 6). As of January 2015, the MLC as has 64 ratifications with a total share of 80 per cent of gross tonnage. This contribution is focused exclusively on the drafting process between 2001 and 2006 and does not discuss implementation (i.e., whether EU member states have punished non-ratifying states through the no-more favourable treatment clause), EU Council co-ordination of the ratification process by member states, or subsequent amendments to the MLC.

There are several reasons why this case has been chosen. Firstly, the relatively limited literature studying the EU's influence over process regulation has mostly focused on environmental policy, and this contribution addresses the under-researched area of social policy regulation. Secondly, as the MLC is a significant addition to maritime regulation, any actor regarded as a regulatory 'great power' would be expected to seek influence over such an instrument. Thirdly, the EU is expected to be less influence in institutional setting where rule-mediated standard-setting take place compared to power-based bargaining situations where the possibility of exclusion exists (Young 2015). The ILO in general, and the MLC negotiations in particular, exemplify a negotiating environment in which EU power is reduced. Firstly, while the EU can in some institutions enjoy more voting power through its member states, in the ILO this is reduced for structural and normative reasons. The tripartite architecture grants workers, employers and government equal voting shares during drafting negotiations, reducing the significance of the EU's combined votes. Moreover, the norm of seeking consensus is especially pronounced in the MLC owing to a strong co-operative ethos between the social partners in the maritime sector and meant parties strive to avoid resorting to voting on contentious issues. Secondly, the EU is more likely to engage in strategic interaction (policies anticipating how others will respond) in reciprocal negotiations such as those of the MLC, requiring it to sometimes accept policies that do not reflect EU preferences, for the sake of consensus. As elaborated below, this has implications for both the position of the EU on the spectrum of preferences, as well as further reducing its bargaining power over other negotiating parties. By using official ILO records to ascertain when the EU spoke, how often and how closely its preferences aligned with other actors, the clearest picture yet is presented of EU influence over the MLC.

There are three important reasons developed in the literature to explain why the EU would seek influence over ILO labour standards. The first is the EU's foreign policy goal to promote effective multilateralism, the United Nations system and international law, and the ILO clearly falls within this remit (Council 2003: 9). Although the EU is not a member of the ILO, the European Commission has officially co-operated with the secretariat of the ILO since 1955, periodically updating, expanding and strengthening its co-operative

THE EUROPEAN UNION AS A GLOBAL REGULATOR?

relationship, most recently in 2001 (Johnson 2005). Originally, co-operation between the ILO and the EU focused exclusively on creating a harmonized social policy among member states (Kissack 2014), but today this has broadened into a wider concern for social standards within development policy (European Commission 2001) and globalization (Orbie and Tortell 2009a). European studies has been interested in international labour standards for almost a decade, drawing together scholarship on the EU in the ILO (Delarue 2006; Kissack 2008, 2009a, 2009b, 2011; Nedergaard 2009; Riddervold 2008, 2010; Riddervold and Sjursen 2012; Saenen and Orbie 2011), conditionality and trade policy (Orbie and Tortell 2009b), and the external impact of EU social policy (Novitz 2009). The second reason derives from the normative nature of the EU as an international actor. Manners's (2002) 'normative power Europe' (NPE) thesis argues that the *sui generis* nature of the EU predisposes it to a foreign policy promoting universal norms and values in the place of national interests. The ILO's work to promote fundamental labour rights, which are also set out in the Universal Declaration of Human Rights (Alston 2005), constitutes part of the corpus of international human rights law that NPE supports (Orbie 2011). Riddervold and Sjursen (2012) argue that the EU promotes human rights through international law as part of a constitution-building process for cosmopolitan rights, drawing on examples of EU co-ordination during MLC negotiations.

The third reason centres on what Orbie and Barbinde (2008: 461) call the 'social-trade nexus': how to reconcile neoliberal economic policies and solidarist social policies both inside and outside the EU. The global trend that began in the 1980s to reduce the size of the state through neoliberal policies of privatization and marketization has led to the creation of isomorphic regulatory regimes supervising liberalized sectors (Levi-Faur 2005). European states have retained many welfare policies designed to counter the negative externalities of liberalization and protect basic standards deemed socially important. However, trade liberalization adversely affects sectors (such as apparel and footwear) that struggle to compete with foreign producers without the cost of implementing the European social model.[2] World Trade Organization rules make it difficult to use product regulation to prevent competition in vulnerable sectors, so one alternative is to develop process regulation in the form of promoting high labour standards beyond EU borders. The EU has diffused these norms through the enlargement process to accession states, and with limited success through external governance mechanisms (Lavenex and Schimmelfennig 2009), diffusion (Börzel and Risse 2012), and its bilateral and regional trade agreements. The ILO's Decent Work campaign to improve working conditions globally makes it an ideal partner for a self-interested EU trying to maintain its competitiveness. The EU offers GSP trade incentives to encourage third states to ratify all eight ILO core labour standards and has suspended trade preferences to serious violators (Orbie and Tortell 2009b), but critics identify inconsistency in the application of penalties and developing states remain suspicious that labour standards are a veil hiding protectionist policies. The MLC was an opportunity for the EU to promote all three of these concerns: international law; improved human rights; and levelling the playing field between European flag states implementing high standards and open register flag states where protection is lower.

EXPLAINING EU INFLUENCE AT THE ILO

In his introduction to this collection, Young (2015) identifies the tendency in the literature to concentrate on ascribing influence over regulatory regimes to EU attributes rather than identifying causal mechanisms, and the following section links the case of the MLC to this collection's common methodology. This case study is an example of regulatory co-operation rather than regulatory diffusion, and the attributes of market size, regulatory stringency and regulatory capacity are expected to be less significant in determining the level of EU influence. Nevertheless, it is useful to briefly consider each in turn as they help contextualize the position of the EU in negotiations. In terms of market size, in 2006 (the year the MLC was concluded), the European Commission (2006: 6) reported that 28 per cent of the total number of ships worldwide were registered in states belonging to the European Economic Area,[3] a significant number but considerably less than the 50 per cent in open register states. In terms of regulatory stringency, many provisions of the MLC fall within EU member state competencies and resulted in different preferences and difficulty acting coherently during the early years of negotiations. Lastly, regulatory capacity is significant in this case because the MLC grants port states that have ratified the convention powers to impound vessels believed to violate standards. Given the large quantity of traded goods exported and imported to the European market, EU states gained 'territorial extension' (Scott 2014) to enforce the MLC on ships registered in non-ratifying states that entered European ports through the 'no more favourable treatment' clause' (ILO 2003: §285), which was accepted in principle from the outset (ILO 2001, §50). Shipowners, wishing to avoid this, applied pressure on flag states to negotiate a convention they would be willing to ratify.

An important distinction between regulatory diffusion and regulatory co-operation is that the latter requires all parties to be actively engaged, while the former can take place unilaterally (i.e., through emulation). Within the MLC negotiations, it is necessary to clarify our assumptions about EU actorness, EU goals and the impact the institutional settings on the capacity of the EU to operate. Addressing actorness first, given the importance of labour market harmonization for European integration, it is unsurprising that EU representation in ILO debates dates back to 1971, when a member of the European Commission addressed the annual conference, and the first Presidency intervention in the name of the European Economic Community (EEC) came in 1973 (Kissack 2008). The 1986 Single European Act created Community competencies in areas of employment policies (e.g., occupational safety and health) that required the Commission to represent member states, but the institutional

THE EUROPEAN UNION AS A GLOBAL REGULATOR?

design of the ILO is built upon national tripartite representation and there remains resistance to enhancing the role of REIOs (ESC 1995). Consequently, EU member states are sometimes forced to negotiate issues that they have formally ceded sovereignty over to the Union level (Cavicchiolo 2002). Efforts by the Commission to take a prominent role in co-ordinating these issues have repeated led to confrontation, the first of which was arbitrated by European Court of Justice Opinion 2/91 (1993). EU member states continue to jealously guard their status as members of the ILO and the Council only mandated the Commission to assist formal co-ordination in the MLC negotiations in April 2005, over four years into the process and 10 months prior to its completion (European Commission 2006: 6). According to Riddervold, since 2003:

> EU co-ordination meetings were held during and in between the ILO meetings, where concrete provisions in the MLC were discussed. The EU members established common positions on all areas of the MLC prior to its final adoption in 2006. (Riddervold 2010: 583)

This article goes beyond existing research by examining EU co-ordination in relation to when key decisions were taken, assessing EU coherence in comparison to the preferences of other negotiating parties, and measuring influence in terms of shaping the text of the MLC.

This contribution draws its empirical data from the ILO's official proceedings, in order to establish when EU common positions were given (degree of EU cohesion), their position in the spectrum of preferences and the impact made. The advantages of this approach are that one can see (a) exactly how often the EU presents common positions; (b) their location in a wider debate and whether they are outliers or represent the median; (c) the positions of member states (if speaking alone) can also be identified and consistency gauged; (d) ILO official records are circulated to participants prior to final publication to ensure accuracy. There are, however, a number of disadvantages, such as (a) focusing on only formal interventions and not green room, unminuted or informal influence; (b) inaccuracy recording when the EU Presidency speaks *qua* sovereign state and when on behalf of the EU; (c) an underrepresentation of co-ordination efforts if there are no concrete outputs to be minuted in the proceedings. The final, and perhaps most important, shortcoming is that not all EU member states attended negotiations in the early years, with landlocked states often absent. Saenen's (2014) detailed analysis of the MLC preparatory meetings records which EU member states attended which meetings and his solution to the problem of how to identify EU actorness in MLC negotiations was to treat an 'EU core group' of member states speaking frequently as a bloc but not in the name of the EU as a proxy, and measure coherence and consistency over time. While this undoubtedly served the purpose of his research, its pragmatic approach to identifying the EU in international negotiations must respond to the criticism that unless decisions are taken through EU institutions and issued in the name of the union, there is no meaningful EU output. To keep

THE EUROPEAN UNION AS A GLOBAL REGULATOR?

within the common methodology of this collection, the strict definition of EU influence deriving from EU interventions as recorded in the official documentation of the ILO is used.

What was the EU trying to achieve at the MLC negotiations? Since many of the conventions being consolidated pre-date EU law, and member states' national law already conforms with the ILO conventions they have ratified, there were few opportunities to upload EU preferences into the MLC. Despite this, the literature identifies three core EU objectives. The first was to ensure that the MLC was a widely ratified convention that would create a level playing field in the place of the inconsistent coverage of the existing maritime labour instruments. Tortell *et al.* (2009: 125) argue that 'an explanation of why the EU was so actively involved in the drafting stage of the MLC and its eventual adoption was to ensure that the EU's norms [of maximal labour standards] ... were projected onto the resulting convention'. The European Commission clearly (2006: 3) articulated this goal, as did many member states. So, too, did both social partners – seafarers unsurprisingly (ILO 2003: §10) and shipowners who, although usually disposed towards lower and/or more flexible standards, recognized that 'a level playing field' for the industry would improve competition and was in the interests of their constituents (ILO 2002: §37, 2004b: §7). The EU's second goal was to maximize the standards codified in the MLC and create a 'seafarers' bill of rights', against opponents' view of the MLC purely as a consolidation exercise. The Netherlands and the UK were two of the strongest proponents of this position from the beginning, and Riddervold (2008: 2) argues 'the EU has been the main promoter of a Convention of high-minimum standards', as co-ordination consolidated a common view of the MLC as a human rights issue. The final goal was to insert an REIO clause in the titles on social security to ensure it was compatible with EU law (European Commission 2006: 6). The convention carefully balanced the duties of flag states and seafarers' national social security systems according to short- and long-term benefits, but EU member states required a waiver from this arrangement for EU citizens working on ships registered in EU states other than their own, which the REIO clause permits. EU influence cannot be doubted in insertion of the REIO clause as it was the only supporter of the proposal and is an example of defensive action preventing international commitments constraining existing EU law and practice.

What is the wider significance of this case in terms of lessons that can travel to the broader debate on EU regulatory influence? Rather than label it either 'hard' or 'easy', it is more accurate to see it as juxtaposing competing expectations. We would expect less EU influence as a result of the ILO's tripartite structure and rules-based procedures. Yet, contrary to this, the importance of the EU as an origin or destination for so many traded goods and the regulatory competency of port states, its status as a regulatory 'great power' and the consensus in the literature suggest that the EU should exert influence. The empirical data presented will determine which is correct, and why.

71

THE EUROPEAN UNION AS A GLOBAL REGULATOR?

ASSESSING EU INFLUENCE IN THE MLC NEGOTIATIONS

This section presents empirical data drawn from official ILO documentation of MLC negotiations over the six years from 2001 to 2006.[4] Influence in the MLC is defined across a continuum from high to low as the ability of an actor to (a) successfully upload a policy preference into the MLC; (b) shift a median position closer to its own preferences; (c) convince others to support its preferences (even if ultimately unsuccessful in mobilizing enough support to shift the median position). While authors such as Saenen (2014) equate blocs of EU member states exerting influence with EU influence, for reasons specified above this contribution concentrates on influence from EU common interventions. Wherever possible an overview of EU member state positions is provided to situate the search for common positions within EU member state preferences. I argue that while the EU undoubtedly became a more coherent actor during negotiations, and successfully influenced a few important issues, this did not amount to significant influence over the content of the MLC because many major issues were decided prior to EU co-ordination. EU influence in five issues is examined: structure; simplified amendment procedure; inspection and enforcement; scope; and social security. The first four were identified by the negotiating parties as of key concern (ILO 2002: §4) and the fifth is social security provision, an issue area where the MLC moves beyond consolidation to new legislation. I argue that many of these issues were fundamentally resolved prior to formal EU co-ordination, and when unresolved issues remained open in the later meetings, the EU was less influential than expected.

Structure

Of the five key issues, the structure of the MLC was the first to be decided. The convention is tiered on four levels, starting with norms and principles in the Articles (level 1), and continues with increasingly detailed technical instructions for implementation in Regulations (level 2), Standards (level 3) and Guidelines (level 4) (ILO 2002: §34). Levels 1–3 are mandatory for all states ratifying the convention and level 4 are non-mandatory. The four-level design, although using different names at the time, was modelled on IMO conventions and agreed by the government group in 2002. The major division between states was over the rigidity of the levels (ILO 2002: §6). South Korea and the Bahamas (an open register state) supported a 'MARPOL-type approach' (ILO 2002: §20, §24) while a more stringent 'STCW-type approach' was preferred by the UK, Denmark (the only two EU member state governments to speak and reveal their preferences), a number of non-EU governments, seafarers and shipowners (ILO 2002: §30–3). The more stringent approach was eventually adopted, and while two EU member states supported it early on, the consensus of the social partners was undoubtedly a more important factor determining the outcome. The EU cannot be said to have influenced this issue, as there was neither EU co-ordination nor representation in 2002, and

THE EUROPEAN UNION AS A GLOBAL REGULATOR?

the UK and Denmark were part of a larger group of governments in favour of the shared preference of seafarers and shipowners.

Simplified amendment procedure

Negotiators spoke of the need for a 'living convention', by which they meant an instrument that could be amended relatively easily, in order to remain up-to-date and relevant to the maritime industry. The primary concern was finding a compromise between imposing too high a threshold for amendment that made change impossible, and too low a threshold that risks fundamentally altering the nature of the convention states initially ratified. The solution was an IMO model that established different rules for 'explicit' modifications to Articles and Regulations (levels 1 and 2) through normal ILO procedures (agreed by ballot at conference) and 'tacit' modifications to Standards and Guidelines (levels 3 and 4) that could be adopted in specially convened technical meetings. The basic principle of a simplified amendment procedure was accepted in 2002 (ILO 2002: §6) and re-affirmed in 2003 (ILO 2003: §170–204), although discussion continued until 2006 about the voting majorities required, the rules on tabling an amendment, and how modified rules would come into effect (ILO 2005b: 9–10). There is insufficient space to consider all aspects, so focus is turned to the question of how many government members must support an amendment seeking to change the MLC in order for it to be considered.

In 2004, the social partners suggested 12 states must support an amendment, to which the 'Government member of Denmark and Chairperson of the Government group cautioned that some governments might find this too high' (ILO 2004a: §171), a view echoed by the Republic of Korea. The following year, the social partners proposed a figure of 10 in the place of 12, while 'Japan proposed a total of five or seven [and] … Korea proposed "1+4"' (ILO 2005a: §50), meaning one state proposing an amendment and four states seconding it. Among the government group '[m]ost had concurred with the position of the social partners (1+9 solution); some had preferred the 1+4 option' (ILO 2005a: §51). With no resolution in sight, at the final negotiation in 2006 a small working group of seafarers, shipowners and 13 states (including Ireland, the Netherlands and the UK) was convened to finalize Article XV of the convention (ILO 2006a: §4). The finalized text read that 'an amendment proposed by a government must have been proposed or supported by at least five governments' (Article XV §2) and was recorded as 'a package deal had been agreed upon which delicately balanced the interests concerned and was a compromise position for the members of each group' (ILO 2006a: §240). More specifically regarding the positions of governments, the representative of China 'speaking on behalf of the Government group said that the proposed text had the unanimous support of the Government group' (ILO 2006a: §246). Tracing influence through the negotiation process reveals that the Korean proposal from 2004 was the one finally agreed and supported by all states,

73

THE EUROPEAN UNION AS A GLOBAL REGULATOR?

representing a shift in the government group away from the 1+9 that 'most' states previously preferred. This is an example of the exertion of influence over the final outcome of the MLC, but by the Republic of Korea rather than the European Union.

Inspection and enforcement

From the outset port states inspections were seen as essential for enforcing the convention. How port authorities would enforce compliance was one of the most contentious issues of the negotiations and there is insufficient space to present anything more than a snapshot of proceedings, albeit an informative one. The example chosen is the negotiation of Standard A5.1.4 relating to 'Inspection and Enforcement', and initially discussed only in very broad terms in 2003. Clearly identifiable positions emerged in September 2004, where the central issue dividing all states (including EU member states) was a preference for looser, procedural rules that granted more flexibility, or maximal protection of seafarers' rights.

> Most governments had preferred the first alternative ... because the consequences of the language of the second alternative when too far. Some government members had favoured the second alternative because it contained the words "serious breach of seafarers' rights"'. (ILO 2004b: §325)

Following the debate reveals that among the explicitly stated national positions, Spain and the UK supported maximal rights and Denmark did not (ILO 2004b: §328–31), and that Malta (not at the time an EU member state) introduced a compromise text that prevented negotiations reaching an impasse (ILO 2004b: §333–47).

In 2005, there was insufficient time to debate all the amendments proposed relating to this issue, and instead each amendment was vetted for tripartite support and only successful ones placed on the agenda for the 2006 negotiations. In this process EU co-ordination was highly visible, with 13 common positions presented in support of tabled amendments and one declaration of an inability to reach a common position (ILO 2005a: §271). Of the 13 amendments supported, five were drafted by the EU and eight were drafted by other governments. EU interests were clearly not aligned with those of shipowners and seafarers, as only one of their drafted amendments received the necessary tripartite support, while five (of the eight) amendments by other governments they supported did receive backing from seafarers and shipowners (ILO 2005a: §349). In 2006, the EU made one common amendment with regard to Standard A5.1.4 §9, with a proposal to lessen the burden of reporting 'unintentional violations' on port states. The UK government justified the amendment, saying 'true breaches [of standards] needed to be recorded, along with the action taken to remedy them. Requiring inspectors to record every exercise of discretion would lead to unnecessary paperwork' (ILO 2006a: §1029). The proposal was opposed by

THE EUROPEAN UNION AS A GLOBAL REGULATOR?

the seafarers' group and partly undermined by the Spanish delegate who admitted the seafarers' 'argument carried weight' and then 'suggested compromise wording' (ILO 2006a: §1033). After further interventions by the France, Germany and the UK, as well as support from other states, shipowners and constructive engagement by seafarers, a reworded version of the EU amendment was adopted (ILO 2006a: §1051).

What influence did the EU have over inspection and enforcement? Firstly, during this period the development of EU co-ordination is evident, from the divergent national positions of 2004 to common EU positions in 2005 and 2006, as expected after the April 2005 Council decision. However, common EU positions did not translate into greater influence. In the 2005 meeting, over one-half of the amendments EU member states agreed to collectively support did not receive the requisite tripartite support for inclusion in the 2006 meeting, and four out of five amendments drafted by the EU fell. Secondly, the empirical evidence does not concur with Riddervold's (2010) argument that EU co-ordination coalesced around seeing the MLC as a human rights issue. Instead, the EU exerted influence to reduce the bureaucratic burden on inspectors, rather than championing seafarers' rights.[5]

Scope

Seafarers' representatives wanted the MLC to cover workers on all commercial vessels, and any restrictions in scope would lead to 'institutionalized maritime apartheid' (ILO 2005a: §12). Conversely, governments wanted to the convention to apply to a minimum size ship. Preliminary drafts suggested a figure of 500 gross tons, and the first detailed discussions on this figure occurred in 2004, during which the UK stated that it 'was of fundamental importance to protect seafarers with this convention' but still advocated size limits because in 'the absence of such limits in some cases would create a serious burden to the governments for regular inspection' (ILO 2004b: §26). The Netherlands, Denmark, Sweden, Germany and France supported this position in their interventions (ILO 2004b: §27–31), as did many other states, including 'a number of government members from the Asia-Pacific group [that] supported the 500 gross ton limit' (ILO 2004b: §38). The issue was returned to in 2005, where the rationale to keep the 500 gross tons limit was 'to make the convention acceptable to member states' (ILO 2005a: §11). As the issue could not be resolved, a tripartite working group composed of seafarers, shipowners, China, Japan, Korea, Norway, UK and US agreed a figure of 200 gross tons (ILO 2005a: §36). The preferences of the parties was not revealed, but from the interventions on this subject it is clear that China (ILO 2004b: §29) Korea (ILO 2004b: §37), the US (ILO 2006a: §604), and employers (ILO 2006: §602) sought a limit of 500, while seafarers preferred 100 and 'had agreed on a compromise figure of 200, which was the maximum that had been acceptable' (ILO 2006a: §603). Two scenarios may explain the setting of the limit at 200 gross tons; either seafarers exerted a considerable amount of influence, or Norway, Japan and the UK

THE EUROPEAN UNION AS A GLOBAL REGULATOR?

(either individually or collectively) also exerted influence in support of the lower limit. While the UK held the EU Presidency at the time and gave the Union a presence in the room, these sources cannot definitively say how much influence the EU had over this.

Social security

One issue immediately stands out in the EU's contribution to the debate over social security: ensuring that the convention did not negatively impact on existing EU law. In 2004, a year before the Council decision authorizing the Commission to assist in co-ordination, the Dutch Presidency and the European Commission spoke on behalf of the EU, confirming expectations of the theory of implied powers. Early into negotiations the Netherlands announced the EU member states 'intended to submit a proposed change related to the relationship between the convention and regional legal instruments ... towards safeguarding existing rights under EU law' (ILO 2004d: §282). Later, the highly unusual step was taken to allow a 'representative of the European Commission' to explain the incompatibility between the convention and EU law and justify the need for an amendment, as it would be difficult for EU member states 'to ratify a convention which could be seen as derogating from European Union law' (ILO 2004d: §378). The solution was to incorporate an amendment proposed by Belgium, Denmark, Germany, Greece and the Netherlands permitting regional economic integration organizations to make 'other rules concerning the social security legislation seafarers are subject to' (ILO 2004d: §356), which was reworded by the drafting committee and became Standard 4.5.§4. The following year in 2005, the discussion on social security focused on technical issues within the guidelines (level 4) and there was no evidence of EU representation (ILO 2005a: §69-82), while in 2006, the entire code (Regulation, Standard and Guidelines) was adopted without amendments (ILO 2006a: §825–7). The inclusion of the REIO clause is an important example of EU influence that was achieved with the support of the social partners and was explicitly presented as an EU common position. The Council Decision of 7 June 2007 followed up on this point, authorizing the ratification of the MLC on the grounds that the member states are 'bound by the Community rules on the co-ordination of social security schemes based on Article 42 of the Treaty to ratify the Convention in the interests of the Community' (Council 2007: §8). Indeed, the credible legal reasons why failure to secure the amendment might lead to non-ratification by EU states may have heightened their influence. However, aside from this, there is little evidence of co-ordinated EU efforts successfully shaping other social security provisions. In summary, Table 1 provides a chronological summary of the key events in the five issue areas considered above.

THE EUROPEAN UNION AS A GLOBAL REGULATOR?

CONCLUSION

This contribution assesses EU influence over the final content of the ILO MLC, intended to be the fourth pillar of the global maritime regulatory regime. The objective of the ILO was to consolidate 67 standards into one 'super-convention' that would greatly increase the coverage and consistency of labour protection in commercial shipping. The EU, as regulatory 'great power', with over 25 per cen of the world fleet registered with its member states, and as a major global trader of goods that travel through European ports, was *prima facia* expected to take a strong interest in shaping the document. ILO official records of negotiations over six years from 2001 to 2006 were used to measure the influence of the EU in five key issues of the MLC: structure, simplified amendment process, inspection and enforcement, scope and social security.

This article argues that the EU was less influential in the negotiation of the MLC than the existing literature maintains, based on process tracing the positions of EU and non-EU actors on the five most important areas of the MLC over six years. No EU voice was heard during the debate on the structure nor simplified amend procedure. On the issue of scope, the EU Presidency participated in the informal working group that reached a compromise, but ILO records are inconclusive about EU influence over therein. Enforcement was an area in which the EU did have impact, although the thrust of its influence reduced the burden on port authority inspectors instead of championing seafarers' rights. Finally, in the area of social security, the inclusion of the REIO clause is a clear example of EU influence, since it serves very clearly its own interest in making the MLC compliant with existing EU law.

There is strong evidence to support the claim that the degree of cohesion between EU member states is important, but insufficient, to exert influence. The need to make the MLC compliant with existing EU social security law was a powerful catalyst for EU co-ordination. Measured by documented interventions in negotiations, the EU appears as a coherent actor for the first time in 2004 in this debate, one year before the Council mandate was granted. More strikingly, it was the only issue on which a European Commission official made an intervention on behalf of the EU, supporting the thesis of implied powers conveying external competence where internal rules might be adversely affected by an international agreement. Conversely, an important part of the explanation for why the EU did not influence several key parts of the MLC is because they were agreed prior to the start of EU co-ordination. While a number of EU member states were undoubtedly influential during the first three years of talks, the EU itself was absence.

As stated at the outset, the EU was rarely a preference outlier in negotiations, flanked on one side by seafarers and open register states on the other. In the early years of negotiations EU member states were divided, with northern states preferring strong rights and Greece, along with Malta and Cyprus preferring looser standards. The existing literature presents the EU as a rights promoter, thus placing it closer to seafarers, and the closest this article's empirical data comes to supporting that claim is the inconclusive records of whether the EU influenced the fixing of the scope of the MLC at 200 gross tons. Evidence to contrary was presented, too, in the case of lessening the enforcement burden on inspectors, explicitly against the wishes of seafarers. Finally, the example of the EU as a policy outlier (REIO clause) was one of successful influence of the MLC, albeit in a provision that only applied to them.

Finally, considerable evidence was found in support of the argument that the ILO, as an example of rules-based negotiations, is an institutional setting that lessens EU influence. The norm of tripartite consensus was strong, which had two important consequences. The first is that it helped negotiate a process regulation that was widely acceptable and in contrast to how process regulation in environmental or social standards is often perceived – as a form of protectionism. The second is that the EU was often located close to the tripartite median position, making it difficult to measure its influence in isolation from other actors. In the empirical examples used, the EU was often unrepresented, divided, or a preference outlier, over-coming this problem. However, it is important to stress that the five issue areas were selected based on their significance to the MLC, not to intention-ally portray the EU negatively. An important task in future research is to look at more MLC issue areas that were less important and where the EU was (potentially) unified and influential, to consider the pays-offs between achiev-ing influence and the significance of influence. Additionally, techniques of tri-angulation through expert interviews with EU and non-EU negotiators could identify forms of EU influence not captured in the formal records. Until more work is done, however, the official records of MLC negotiations do not provide convincing evidence that the EU was a great power in shipping's fourth regulatory pillar.

Biographical note: Robert Kissack is an assistant professor and head of studies at the Institut Barcelona d'Estudis Internacionals (IBEI). He completed his PhD at the London School of Economics in 2006, and has been at IBEI since 2008. His main research area is European foreign policy in multilateral institutions, International Relations theory and international organizations.

ACKNOWLEDGEMENTS

I would like to thank Alasdair Young, the participants of the 'Regulatory Power Europe? Assessing the EU's Efforts to Shape Global Rules' workshop in Georgia Tech, Atlanta, 18–19 April 2014 (funded by Jean Monnet Chair 2012-3121), and two anonymous reviewers for their extremely helpful comments on earlier versions of this contribution.

THE EUROPEAN UNION AS A GLOBAL REGULATOR?

NOTES

1 The practice of registering merchant ships owned by foreign companies is termed 'open register' or 'flag of convenience' and is usually done because of such states have lower regulatory standards.

2 The European social model is codified in Title IV (Solidarity) of the Charter of Fundamental Rights of the European Union, regarding freedom of association and collective bargaining, fair treatment and equal opportunities, minimum ages, upholding health and safety laws, provision of social security and parental leave.

3 The EEA is cited in European Commission reports because Norway and Iceland participated closely in the final stages of EU coordination, and both have sizable fleets – Norway's fleet is the same size as that of France.

4 These were the final reports of the *High-level Tripartite Working Group on Maritime Labour Standards* (TWGMLS) from 2001 to 2004 (ILO 2001, 2002, 2003, 2004a), two reports of the *Preparatory Technical Maritime Conference* (PTMC) (ILO 2004b, 2004c, 2004d), three reports of the *Tripartite Intersessional Meeting on the Follow-up to the Preparatory Technical Maritime Conference* (TIM) (ILO 2005a, 2005b), and the *Report of the Committee of the Whole* at the 2006 Maritime International Labour Conference (ILO 2006a).

5 The other major EU drafted amendment in Title 5 (Compliance and enforcement) was in Regulation 5.2.1 where the EU, with Norway, Iceland, Bulgaria and Romania, proposed reducing the burden on inspectors to pass details of minor violations onto other port authorities (ILO 2006a: §1101). Instead, they proposed integrating into an existing regulatory system called EQUASIS. While receiving support from many governments and shipowners, the EU was forced to accept a revised text to secure seafarers' support that 'differed significantly from the original amendment and would involve an additional burden for seafarers, shipowners, flag states and port states' (ILO 2006a: §1124).

REFERENCES

Alston, P. (2005) 'Labour rights as human rights: the not so happy state of the art' in P. Alston, *et al* (eds), *Labour Rights as Human Rights*, Oxford: Oxford University Press, pp. 1–25.

Börzel, T. and Risse, T. (2012) 'From Europeanization to diffusion: introduction', *West European Politics* 35(1): 1–19.

Cavicchiolo, L. (2002) 'The relations between the European Community and the International Labour Organisation', in E. Cannizzaro (ed.), *The European Union as an Actor in International Relations*, The Hague: Kluwer Law International, pp. 261–9.

Council (2003) *A Secure Europe in a Better World: European Security Strategy*, Brussels, 12 December 2003.

Council (2007) 'Council decision authorising member states to ratify, in the interests of the European Community, the Maritime Labour Convention, 2006, of the International Labour Organisation', *2007/431/EC*, 7 June 2007, Brussels.

Damro, C. (2012) 'Market power Europe,' *Journal of European Public Policy* 19(5): 682–99.

della Porta, D. (2008) 'Comparative analysis: case-oriented versus variable-oriented research', in D. della Porta and M. Keating (eds), *Approaches and Methodologies in the Social Sciences: A Pluralistic Perspective*, Cambridge: Cambridge University Press, pp. 198–222.

Delarue, R. (2006) 'ILO–EU cooperation on employment and social affairs', in J. Wouters, F. Hoffmeister and T. Ruys (eds), *The United Nations and the European Union. An Ever Closer Partnership*, The Hague: TMC Asser Press, pp. 93–114.

THE EUROPEAN UNION AS A GLOBAL REGULATOR?

Drezner, D.W. (2007) *All Politics is Global: Explaining International Regulatory Regimes*, Princeton, NJ: Princeton University Press.

ECJ (1993) 'Opinion 2/91: Convention N° 170 of the International Labour Organization concerning safety in the use of chemicals at work', *OJ C109*, Brussels, 19 April.

ESC (1995) 'Own-Initiative opinion on: relations between the EU and the International Labour Organisation', *CES 46/95*, Brussels.

European Commission (2001) 'Promoting core labour standards and improving social governance in the context of globalisation, *COM (2001) 416 final*, Brussels, 18 June.

European Commission (2006) 'Communication from the Commission under Article 138(2) of the EC Treaty on the strengthening of maritime labour standards', *COM (2006) 287 final*, Brussels, 15 June.

ILO (2001) 'Final report', *TWGMLS/2001/10*, Geneva: International Labour Organization.

ILO (2002) 'Final report', *TWGMLS/2002/13*, Geneva: International Labour Organization.

ILO (2003) 'Final report', *TWGMLS/2003/10*, Geneva: International Labour Organization.

ILO (2004a) 'Final report', *TWGMLS/2004/19*, Geneva: International Labour Organization.

ILO (2004b) 'Preparatory technical maritime conference, report of Committee No. 1', *PTMC/04/3-1*, Geneva: International Labour Organization.

ILO (2004c) 'Preparatory technical maritime conference, report of Committee No. 2', *PTMC/04/3-2*, Geneva: International Labour Organization.

ILO (2004d) 'Preparatory technical maritime conference, report of Committee No. 3', *PTMC/04/3-3*, Geneva: International Labour Organization.

ILO (2005a) 'Report of the discussion', *PTMC/2005/23*, Geneva: International Labour Organization.

ILO (2005b) 'Unresolved issues for the draft consolidated maritime labour Convention 2006', *PTMC/2005/1*, Geneva: International Labour Organization.

ILO (2006a) *Provisional Record 7 Part I Report of the Committee Of the Whole*, Geneva: International Labour Organization.

ILO (2006b) *Provisional Record 7 Part II Proposed Consolidated Maritime Labour Convention*, Geneva: International Labour Organization.

Johnson, A. (2005) *European Welfare States and Supranational Governance of Social Policy*, Basingstoke: Palgrave.

Kissack, R. (2008) 'EU actorness in the International Labour Organisation: comparing declaratory and voting cohesion', *Global Society* 22(4): 469–89.

Kissack, R. (2009a) 'How to lose friends and alienate people? The EU as a global social power', *European Journal of Social Policy* 19(2): 99–116.

Kissack, R. (2009b) 'Writing a new normative standard? EU member states and the drafting and ratification of ILO labour standards', in J. Orbie and L. Tortell (eds), *The European Union's Role in the World and the Social Dimension of Globalisation*, London: Routledge, pp. 98–112.

Kissack, R. (2011) The EU's performance in the International Labour Organization', *Journal of European Integration* 33(6): 651–65.

Kissack, R. (2014) 'A changing role for the ILO in the EU promotion of labour standards over time: consistency and EU institutional evolution', in A. Orsini (ed.), *The European Union With(in) International Organisations: Continuity, Commitment and Consistency*, Aldershot: Ashgate, pp. 75–94.

Lavenex, S. and Schimmelfennig, F. (2009) 'EU rules beyond EU borders: theorising external governance in European politics', *Journal of European Public Policy* 16(6): 791–812.

THE EUROPEAN UNION AS A GLOBAL REGULATOR?

Lazer, D. (2006) 'Global and domestic governance: modes of interdependence in regulatory policymaking' *European Law Journal*, (12)4: 455–68.

Levi-Faur, D. (2005) 'The global diffusion of regulatory capitalism', *The Annals of the American Academy* 598: 12–32.

Manners, I. (2002) 'Normative power Europe: a contradiction in terms?', *Journal of Common Market Studies* (40)2: 235–58.

Nedergaard, P. 2009. 'The European Union at the ILO's international labour conferences: a "double" principal–agent analysis', in K.E. Jørgensen (ed.), *The European Union and International Organizations*, London: Routledge, pp.149–66.

Novitz, T. (2009) 'In search of a coherent social policy: EU import and export of ILO labour standards?', in J. Orbie and L. Torrell (eds), *The European Union's Role in the World and the Social Dimension of Globalisation*, London: Routledge, pp. 27–44.

Orbie, J. (2011) 'Promoting labour standards through trade: normative power or regulatory state Europe?', in R. Whitman (ed.), *Normative Power Europe: Empirical and Theoretical Perspectives*, Basingstoke: Palgrave, pp. 160–83.

Orbie, J. and Babarinde, O. (2008) 'The social dimension of globalization and EU development policy: promoting core labour standards and corporate social responsibility', *Journal of European Integration* 30(2): 459–77.

Orbie, J. and Tortell, L. (2009a) 'From the social clause to the social dimension of globalization', in J. Orbie and L. Torrell (eds), *The European Union's Role in the World and the Social Dimension of Globalisation*, London: Routledge, pp. 1–26.

Orbie, J. and Tortell, L. (2009b) 'The new GSP+ beneficiaries: ticking the box or truly consistent with ILO findings?', *European Foreign Affairs Review* 14(3): 663–81.

Riddervold, M. (2008) 'Interests or principles? EU foreign policy in the ILO?', *RECON Online Working Paper 2008/09*, ARENA.

Riddervold, M. (2010) 'A matter of principle? EU foreign policy in the International Labour Organization', *Journal of European Public Policy* 17(4): 581–98.

Riddervold, M. and Sjursen, H. (2012) 'Playing into the hands of the Commission? The case of EU coordination in the ILO', in O. Costa and K.E. Jørgensen (eds), *The Influence of International Institutions on the European Union: When Multilateralism hits Brussels*, Basingstoke: Palgrave, pp. 42–57.

Saenen, B. (2014) 'The causal relation between the European Union's coherence and effectiveness in international institutions: the Union in the standard-setting procedure of the International Labour Organization', PhD thesis, University of Ghent, Ghent.

Saenen, B. and Orbie, J. (2011) 'Challenges to coherence: exploring the European Union's role in the International Labour Organization', in J. Lieb, N. von Ondarza and D. Schwarzer (eds), *The EU in International Fora. Lessons for the Union's External Representation after Lisbon*, Baden-Baden: Nomos, pp. 159–74

Scott, J. (2014) 'Extraterritoriality and territorial extension in EU Law', *American Journal of Comparative Law*, 62: 87–126.

Tortell, L., Delarue, R. and Kenner, J. (2009) 'The EU and the ILO Maritime Labour Convention', in J. Orbie and L. Tortell (eds), *The European Union's Role in the World and the Social Dimension of Globalisation*, London: Routledge, pp. 113–30.

Young, A.R. (2015) 'The European Union as a global regulator? Context and comparison', *Journal of European Public Policy*, doi: 10.1080/13501763.2015.1046902.

THE EUROPEAN UNION AS A GLOBAL REGULATOR?

for polities competing to attract investment and economic activity and for corporate strategy, as companies are frequently forced to absorb sizable costs as they adjust to international rules. Global standards, moreover, can upend long-standing consumer protections and redefine the relationship between governments and their citizens (Newman 2008).

It should thus not be surprising that scholars and policy analysts of the European Union (EU) have turned their attention to the polity's role in global regulation (Bretherton and Vogler 1999; Jacoby and Meunier 2010; Lavenex and Schimmelfennig 2009; Lütz 2011; Müller *et al.* 2014; Vogel 2012). Despite a proliferation of studies on topics ranging from agriculture to finance, the findings of this growing literature can seem wildly disconnected. On the one hand, research has trumpeted the EU's influence, emphasizing, alternatively, the ideas and values that animate EU efforts or power resources rooted in the size and institutional configurations of its internal market (Bradford 2012; Damro 2012; Falkner 2007; Manners 2006). On the other hand, a significant literature details the limits of EU efforts, pointing to its failure to shape global rules in high-profile issue areas (Bretherton and Vogler 2013; Leblond 2011; Sbragia 2010; Young 2014). The skeptics argue that even in cases where the EU has clear preferences (consistent with its reputation as a soft and normative power) and bargaining leverage because of well-developed markets and capacities, such as in the genetically modified organisms (GMOs) dispute, it has not always been able to assert its interests globally or even to adopt strategies towards that end (Pollack and Shaffer 2009). How, then, can we reconcile such conflicting findings?

This contribution's answer turns on the broader *global regulatory context* (Copelovitch and Putnam 2014; Falleti and Lynch 2009; Weber 1994), variance within which conditions EU foreign regulatory strategies and behavior. Thus, while not making predictions about EU influence over specific outcomes *per se* (that is, when it will be able to achieve its goal of being a rule-maker, a rule-blocker, or a rule-taker [Young 2015a]), the contribution looks to the global regulatory context to deduce scope conditions under which the EU can (or cannot) be expected to adopt different policy strategies. Such strategies are the means by which the EU attempts to realize its preferences, given a particular regulatory context (Frieden 1999). The contribution thus connects arguments about the power resources of the EU to the political process of international negotiation and co-operation.

We define the regulatory context as the socio-political setting in a given period of time, which bounds, shapes and constitutes causal connections between the exercise of authority and global rule-making (Falleti and Lynch 2009). For theoretical and empirical reasons developed below, we narrow in on two institutional features of the global regulatory context: the distribution of regulatory capacity across the major economies, and institutional density at the global level. In contrast to the typical treatment of regional institutional arrangements in the literature on the EU as a global actor, we maintain that regulatory capacity is a relational concept. That is to say, it is not solely an

THE EUROPEAN UNION AS A GLOBAL REGULATOR?

EU attribute, but rather a property of the 'system' and properly defined in terms of its international distribution (Bach and Newman 2007, 2010). At the same time, the setting in which the EU engages other regulatory actors varies considerably by forum and mode (traditional international organizations, informal networks, extraterritorial competitive bargaining) and degree and type of agreed rules (non-binding soft law, binding international agreements); as the locus of rule-making shifts and the rule density and type change, the strategies employed by the EU to shape global rules ought to vary (Axelrod and Keohane 1985; Ruggie 1998).

Moving beyond arguments maintaining that the EU 'matters' in a uniform and static way, our study, a largely deductive exercise, identifies potential causal linkages between context and strategies, and suggests that as the context changes, so too does the EU's foreign regulatory engagement. The contribution's core, then, develops an analytic framework that predicts different strategies under alternate conditions and indicates how shifts in these conditions are likely to alter strategies (George and Bennett 2005). In particular, we posit that variation in the regulatory context are likely to result in four distinct strategies: *regulatory export; first-mover agenda-setting; mutual recognition;* and *coalition-building.* In instances, for example, of a large gap in regulatory capacity between the great powers, the EU is more likely to engage in rule projection strategies such as regulatory export or first-mover agenda-setting. Alternatively, high institutional density in concert with parity in regulatory capacity can constrain such rule projection strategies, creating incentives for the EU to move to more negotiated interactions with regulatory partners. The analytic exercise helps identify both sources of and constraints on potential EU behavior as the polity engages in the politics of global regulation (Young 2015a). Given the collection's focus on the role of the EU in influencing global regulation, we limit our empirical illustrations to examples that involve the European polity. That said, our analytic framework could in principle be extended to explain the strategies of other regulatory great powers such as the United States or potentially China.

Our synthetic approach, moreover, unifies a number of existing theoretical arguments about rival standards, first-mover advantages, and regulatory export into a single framework (Drezner 2007; Mattli and Büthe 2003, Quaglia 2014). It also highlights the limits of existing literature that pits various power resources (normative or civilian power) against one another to explain EU influence. Such resources do not operate in opposition but are integrated and embedded in the broader regulatory context. Moreover, a focus on power resources alone ignores the international political context through which such resources get filtered as polities engage with one another and attempt to achieve their policy goals. Finally, the contribution contributes to a growing literature in international relations (IR), comparative politics and European studies highlighting the role of context for conditioning causal relationships (Copelovitch and Putnam 2014; Falleti and Lynch 2009; Müller *et al.* 2014). Ultimately, our analytic approach focusing on the role that context plays in shaping EU policy strategies offers a more nuanced and tractable set of expectations regarding the debate on the EU as a global actor.

The contribution proceeds in four parts. First, we briefly lay out the stakes involved in global regulatory debates. Second, we review the relevant literature on EU power, emphasizing the empirical puzzles. Third, we develop the framework described above, from which we derive a typology of expected EU strategies. Finally, we conclude with implications for research on the EU as a global actor, as well as international relations theory about time, context and causal relationships.

THE EU AS A REGULATORY HEGEMON? CIVILIAN AND NORMATIVE POWER

With the increase in cross-national economic interdependence, regulation has moved to the center stage of the international political economy. As people, goods and information cross borders, multiple states have jurisdictional claims over their behavior. On the one hand, this can produce intense regulatory conflicts, in which states make competing claims over the rules that govern these global markets (Mattli and Woods 2009; Newman and Posner 2011). Such disputes have emerged in a growing range of sectors and issue areas such as chemicals, banking, food, aviation and the Internet to name a few. On the other hand, there is pressure to resolve these conflicts so as to facilitate further globalization. Regulatory co-operation, however, is complicated by the fact that many national regulations were created prior to globalization, and as a result co-ordination requires considerable distributional adjustments by those states with rules different from the global ones (Farrell and Newman 2010; Mattli and Büthe 2003). The ability to set the terms of global regulations, then, becomes an important advantage for domestic firms competing internationally.

A burgeoning literature has singled out the EU as playing a disproportionate role in global contests over rules governing international business. From data privacy to chemicals, the EU has been able to set the global agenda and persuade other countries to adjust their own domestic rules to reflect EU standards (Bach and Newman 2007). This has led scholars like Annu Bradford and Chad Damro to coin terms like the 'Brussels effect' and 'market power Europe' to capture growing European power (Bradford 2012; Damro 2012, 2015).

Approaches to EU global regulatory behavior tend to fall into explanations based on civilian or normative power. The first, locates EU power largely in the development of the internal market and the introduction of the single currency (Bradford 2012; Bretherton and Vogler 1999; Damro 2015; McNamara and Meunier 2002). According to this line of argumentation, the EU has grown to be a second, relatively equal, regulatory power alongside the United States (US). Following the logic of James and Lake's (1989) 'Second face of hegemony' or David Vogel's (1995) *Trading Up*, firms hoping to compete in the European market must follow European rules. This creates competitive pressure on export-oriented and foreign-sales-reliant businesses to lobby their home markets to converge on European rules so as to minimize the transaction costs of following multiple regulatory rulebooks. In contrast to this more passive channel, the EU at times actively exploits the potential extraterritorial reach of its rules so as to shape the behavior of political and market actors (Lavenex and Schimmelfennig 2009). Equivalency clauses in EU legislation are the clearest example, as they condition market access on the demonstration of equivalent rules in home markets. In terms of empirical expectations, civilian power arguments expect that as integration unifies disparate national markets, it provides the EU with a powerful 'single voice'.

Normative power arguments, by contrast, pay less attention to the economic and institutional weight of the European market and more to the ideas that animate EU integration – democracy, human rights, rule of law and modes of co-operation (Bicchi 2006; Laïdi 2008; Manners 2006). In such accounts, the EU leads by being an example of a peaceful, rule-driven society. States, particularly in the periphery of Central and Eastern Europe, emulate EU approaches and standards in order to be seen as viable members of the Western political order. Moreover, the EU has the ability to construct the given by defining types of appropriate behavior that may diffuse through economic, political and societal linkages from the EU to other societies (McNamara 2015).

Civilian and normative power explanations have added to our understanding of the EU's importance in global regulation. In particular, they identify two distinct power resources from which the EU may benefit. First, the integration of the European market creates a powerful cost–benefit incentive for actors in other jurisdiction to adjust to European rules. Market access requirements and trading-up dynamics mean that EU regulations can shape the reversion point of global regulation – the character of the *status quo* absent co-ordination (Gruber 2000; Richards 1999). Once the EU alters its rules, the economic reality of globally active firms shift as they either have to comply with EU rules or suffer the transaction costs associated with complying with multiple rules across jurisdictions. Second, the EU frequently enjoys agenda-setting powers whereby it can define the terms of the rules under discussion. At times, such powers are used to develop and promote specific policy proposals, but they can also be used to forge the background conditions of what is viewed as legitimate. In short, the EU can alter the costs and benefits, as well as the terms around which co-ordination may occur.

Despite focusing attention on the coercive power of the European market and the EU's agenda-setting authority, these approaches suffer from two main weaknesses. The first concerns the tendency to focus on a limited set of possible EU goals and strategies (Müller *et al.* 2014; Young, 2015a). Civilian power approaches tend to emphasize EU efforts to win foreign conformity with its models and standards or to gain first-mover advantages; whereas, normative arguments tend to emphasize diffusion processes. Powerful regulators like the EU serve as 'teachers' to the rest of the world (Finnemore 1996) and, in particular, the exemplar of co-operation techniques and strategies, such as mutual

THE EUROPEAN UNION AS A GLOBAL REGULATOR?

recognition, peer reviews and experimentalist governance architectures (de Búrca 2013; Sabel and Zeitlin 2010). Moreover, neither approach devotes much attention to other possible outcomes, such as transnational coalitions between EU actors and those in other societies (Andonova 2004; Risse-Kappen 1994). We seek a single framework that would offer explanations for a fuller range of observed outcomes.

Second, we join other critics who have had no difficulty poking holes in both civilian and normative power explanations by identifying non-conforming cases (Bretherton and Vogler 2013; Pollack and Shaffer 2009; Young 2014, 2015b). The larger point, in our view, is that the EU-as-a-global-power explanations tend to take reductionist and monocausal approaches. That is, they gauge the EU's internal power resources in relative isolation from factors outside the polity (that is the reductionist part) and focus on their favored causal variable, civilian or normative power (that is the monocausal part). In fact, the current debate unnecessarily creates a dichotomy between different power resources, ignoring important points of interaction between substantive norms and institutions of regulation. Moreover, these approaches frequently equate power resources with influence over outcomes, largely ignoring the political processes that filter and shape the effectiveness of such resources. The result is a frequent overestimation of EU influence and an inability to make sense of important empirical observations such as variance in EU authority across time and sector, cases in which the EU initially had little influence but later found its voice (Posner 2009), or the failure of influence despite a large market and distinct norms, such as in the case of GMOs or food safety (Pollack and Shaffer 2009; Young 2014). In fact, there has been a growing body of research highlighting the varying nature of EU influence across regulatory domains.

THE ROLE OF GLOBAL REGULATORY CONTEXT

Seeking explanations for these empirical puzzles and the wide range of observations, we develop a framework that deduces scope conditions of EU external regulatory behavior from different configurations within the global regulatory context. We accept the potential constitutive role of context. Yet, for the analytic purposes of this contribution, we focus on strategies as used in the strategic actor literature. Such strategies are the:

> ways to obtain ... goals, paths to their preferences. These paths must take into account the environment – other actors and their expected behavior, available information, power disparities. Given this strategic setting, strategies are tools the agent uses to get as close to its preferences as possible. (Frieden 1999: 45)

While the EU may enjoy a variety of power resources, the ability to deploy them and their potential effect are conditioned by the strategic context (Frieden 1999). In other words, a focus on strategies allows us to consider the means by which the EU attempts to achieve its policy goals.

THE EUROPEAN UNION AS A GLOBAL REGULATOR?

Our approach thus contextualizes EU power resources within the larger socio-political setting. By incorporating some of the relational, environmental and temporal components of authority, we extend the recent turn toward institutional context among historical institutionalists, as well as the call by EU scholars, to think more systematically about the interaction between the EU and its global engagements (Falleti and Lynch 2009; Müller *et al.* 2014). We also note that the approach harks back to two insights long made in international relations (IR) theory: that the behavior of powerful countries cannot be understood in isolation, but rather needs to be examined within the political system of interacting great powers (Oatley 2011; Waltz 1979); and that power is context specific and cannot be assessed in universal terms (Jervis 1997; Wendt 1998).

While the global regulatory context could include a range of socio-political factors, in this first exercise we highlight two institutional features that existing research suggests should be particularly important: the distribution of regulatory capacity and the density of institutionalization. In considering variance in these two dimensions of the regulatory context, we deduce a set of likely EU policy strategies. The results of the analytic typology synthesize bodies of research frequently treated separately and in parallel and offer insight into the limits and constraints on EU authority. In the conclusion, we consider a number of extensions that consider other factors associated with the global regulatory context.

Relative differences in regulatory capacity

The two dimensions featured in our contextualization of the EU's external regulatory behavior (the relative capacities of great powers and the international density of rules and institutions) are the core variables in distinct literatures. By taking the *ratio of regulatory capacity* among the major economic powers seriously, we extend that portion of the research on EU market power that already takes a relational approach (Drezner 2007; Simmons 2001). The central idea is that the number of jurisdictions with large markets in a given sector and the relative size of the EU market compared to other such rule-makers are driving forces of external regulatory behavior. Polarity (to use the IR parlance) refers to whether there is a dominant jurisdiction (unipolarity or hegemony), two relatively equal players whose markets are significantly larger than the rest (a bipolar sector), or three or more great regulatory powers (multipolarity). For example, the deep and liquid trading platforms in the US gave its regulators a source of unparalleled market power in finance up through the 1990s (Simmons 2001). With regulatory integration of financial markets in Europe (including London), the EU began to rival US authority (Drezner 2007; Posner 2009). In the post-crisis era and with the emergence of alternate trading venues in Asia and the Middle East, some have wondered whether finance is entering a multipolar phase.

The market power label has become a misnomer, as this literature has taken a decisive institutionalist turn, captured in the concept of regulatory capacity (Bach and Newman 2007; Quaglia 2014; Posner 2009). An increasing body of research demonstrates that relative market size (even the relative portion of

THE EUROPEAN UNION AS A GLOBAL REGULATOR?

international participants in a given market) alone is not a sufficient predictor of regulatory bargaining leverage or influence. Rather, to harness market size, a polity must have the regulatory capacity to define, monitor and defend a specific set of market rules (Bach and Newman 2007; Newman 2008). In other words, a polity must have the institutional expertise, internal arrangements and governance mechanisms to develop a set of rules, identify breaches in those rules and sanction non-compliance. The United States, for example, has a large market for cosmetics but, because of a quirk of legislative history, has few regulatory institutions with authority to oversee that market, let alone export them to other jurisdictions (Bach and Newman 2010). As a result, the regulators of this relatively large market enjoy few advantages in global regulatory debates. A similar finding has been made in insurance and other sectors (Quaglia 2013, 2014). The regulatory capacity approach subsumes both normative and civilian market power arguments to the extent that it identifies areas in which a polity has a substantively distinct regulatory apparatus as well as the institutions to monitor and defend those substantive rules.

Additionally, a polity's regulatory capacity is relative to other rule-making jurisdictions. It is not enough to examine the regulatory institutions of the EU in isolation. Rather, the analysis must consider how they relate to similar ones in other regulatory powers such as the US – first, in terms of institutional development, but also the latter's timing, as research reveals the frequency of first-mover advantages. The EU, for example, has had considerable influence in shaping global debates over Internet privacy because of the absence of regulatory institutions in the US (Newman 2008). Similarly, the EU was long handicapped in global financial debates in part because of the fragmented and self-regulatory nature of oversight in markets such as Germany and the United Kingdom up through the early 1990s (Posner 2009). Thus, because the distribution of regulatory capacity among the major regulatory players has been shown to be an important determinant of how great powers seek to manage regulatory differences and a critical component of the global regulatory context, we use it as one of the two core dimensions of our framework.

Institutional density

Institutional density is the second dimension of the global regulatory context explored. In answer to the question how great powers go about smoothing the regulatory bumps of globalization, the wide-ranging research on the institutionalization of international regulatory space points to an expansive set of pathways by which institutions shape the behavior of the great powers and contribute to their efforts to co-ordinate rules, overcome distributional conflict and, ultimately, facilitate cross-border economic activity (Axelrod and Keohane 1985; Büthe and Mattli 2011; Keohane 1984; Mattli and Woods 2009; Ruggie 1998). In short, the main premise is that whether and how frictions are resolved is in large part contingent on the institutional setting. Depending on the particular theoretical perspective, the institutional environment is seen to

THE EUROPEAN UNION AS A GLOBAL REGULATOR?

channel, structure, reconstitute or constrain the behavior of powerful actors, offering in return the benefits of ensuring commitment, reducing uncertainty and informational asymmetries, and changing preferences and strategies, as well as the contours of internal political contests.

In some areas, institutionalization is considerable as regulation proceeds through treaty-based international bodies that enjoy some degree of formal rule-making and rule-enforcing authority. The WTO's role in the dispute over genetically modified organisms offers the quintessential example. But in many regulatory domains, such formal institutions do not exist. In these cases, global rules are set through soft law regulatory networks. These collections of regulatory authorities, which may be public or private, co-operate transnationally to develop best practices for market behavior. At times, the standards developed are embedded within the domestic law of large markets or adopted and enforced by treaty-based international organizations or private monitoring organizations. The network members meet routinely, follow agreed procedures, monitor compliance and often enjoy considerable rule-making authority; but they tend to have few formal enforcement powers of their own. Research on such networks tends to view them as a fast and flexible alternative to more cumbersome formal co-operation (Green 2014; Porter 2005; Slaughter 2004). Skeptics see their utility limited to simple co-operation problems where there are few distributional consequences (Abbott and Snidal 2000). We emphasize a third perspective: the forums housing the networks have become rule-making arenas where the outcomes have salient distributive effects. Thus, it can matter a great deal who sets the agenda and who gets the rules they want.

Finally, in some instances, the density of regulatory institutions at the global level is extremely weak. There are no formal international organizations and no active regulatory networks, public or private.

EU policy strategies given the global regulatory context: an analytic typology

In this section, we put forth a framework that deduces propositions and captures the interaction effects of relative capacity and institutional density. It suggests that differences in the global regulatory context alter – in patterned ways – the causal impact of institutions and power on regulation-making outcomes of importance. We identify the role of different global regulatory contexts in determining four distinct and widely observed strategies of powerful regulators: exporting home regulation; winning first-mover advantages; forging mutual recognition; and building coalitions. These strategies demonstrate the limits and opportunities associated with regulatory power at the global level and help to resolve empirical puzzles and to fill holes in the existing literature.

The framework outlined in Figure 1 isolates the two primary dimensions of the global regulatory context discussed above. We make a few simplifying assumptions for analytical purposes. First, while future iterations of the framework could expand the number of powerful actors, we focus here on instances

THE EUROPEAN UNION AS A GLOBAL REGULATOR?

		Density of International Institutions	
		Low	High
Relative Regulatory Capacity among Great Powers	Capacity Gap	Regulatory Export	First-Mover
	Capacity Parity	Mutual Recognition	Coalition Building

Figure 1 Policy strategies given variation in global regulatory context

when there are two primary potential rule-makers. Starting with a bipolar world also reflects contemporary reality in most areas of international regulation (Drezner 2007). Second, we assume preference divergence among the regulatory actors. The assumption allows us to highlight cases where simple co-ordination is most difficult and where high switching costs are likely to raise the stakes of the strategic use of power. Third, in the real world, the various strategies discussed below often overlap and are used simultaneously. By treating strategies as if the EU employs them one at a time, we are better able to isolate the causal processes at work.

In terms of regulatory capacity, we imagine a continuum in which the relative distribution of institutional capacities can range from a significant gap to parity. Similarly, density of international institutions range from less densely institutionalized where there are few institutions that exist capable of rule-development or rule-enforcement to more densely institutionalized where there are clear rules at the global level concerning decision-making and implementation.

We posit that the four combinations of this two dimensional regulatory context create different incentives for the external strategies of the regulatory players: regulatory export; first-mover bids; mutual recognition regimes; and coalition building. We derive four hypotheses and develop them in the following section:

H1: The lower the density of international institutions and the larger the gap of relative regulatory capacity among great powers, the more likely the EU adopts a strategy of regulatory export.

H2: The lower the density of international institutions and the smaller the gap of relative regulatory capacity among great powers, the more likely the EU adopts a strategy of mutual recognition.

H3: The higher the density of international institutions and the larger the gap of relative regulatory capacity among great powers, the more likely the EU adopts a first-mover strategy.

THE EUROPEAN UNION AS A GLOBAL REGULATOR?

H4: The higher the density of international institutions and the smaller the gap of relative regulatory capacity among great powers, the more likely the EU adopts a strategy of coalition building.

Regulatory export

In cases where there exists a large gap in regulatory capacities between two regulatory authorities and the international regulatory environment is less densely institutionalized, then the actor with greater regulatory capacity is well positioned to follow a strategy of regulatory export. Given the lack of another actor capable of defining, extending and defending an alternative approach and the lack of an international institutional environment to serve as a constraint, the better endowed regulator is likely to see itself well positioned to promote its own domestic standards globally (Lavenex and Schimmelfennig 2009; Newman 2008). The strategy might include market access rules that contain extraterritorial provisions. The European Union frequently employs these under the label of 'equivalency' clauses. Such rules prohibit participation by foreign firms within the EU's internal market unless their home jurisdictions have similar rules and enforcement deemed (by the EU) as equivalent. The extra-territorial provisions can create asymmetrical negotiating leverage and a trading up dynamic, as foreign firms face a competitive disadvantage in European markets based on their domestic regulatory setting (Birchfield 2015; Young 2003, 2015b). Equivalence provisions thus incentivize internationally active firms to press for regulatory reform at home.

This quadrant is the regulatory context that is often assumed by those that champion EU regulatory power. Given the sparse international institutionalization, large disparity in regulatory capacities is the primary source of strategic incentives. In Gruber's (2000) terms, the EU enjoys the go-it-alone authority to alter the reversion point of global regulation. While a few prominent cases – for example, the environment and chemicals – have received a lot of attention (Falkner 2007; Kelemen and Vogel 2010), we know that few regulatory domains are characterized by this dynamic. Focusing on the regulatory context, thus, helps better articulate the scope conditions for such unilateral pressure.

First-mover agenda setting

Globalization creates considerable uncertainty, as market actors are subject to multiple and overlapping rules. International standards may resolve many of these uncertainties by serving as co-ordination mechanisms and by providing a level playing field for global competition. When authorities believe future transnational standards, codes and guidelines are potentially salient and sticky

THE EUROPEAN UNION AS A GLOBAL REGULATOR?

(that is, once rules are in place, actors have disincentives to change them), they will want to minimize domestic adjustment costs and thereby have incentive to shape them and the organizations and processes that create them (Lall 2014). We posit that, under conditions of dense international institutionalization, regulators with relatively strong capacities will be tempted to pursue a strategy to win first-mover advantages and set the agenda of such international forum.

Here, international institutionalization catalyzes a particular dimension of regulatory capacity – relative institutional complementarities. Mattli and Büthe (2003) argue that the level of institutional complementarities between domestic and international institutions conditions the ability of a regulatory actor to play the role of first-mover. International rule-making forums and bodies follow a wide variety of decision-making rules and procedures. In terms of decision-making rules, for example, some international bodies operate under the one-country, one-vote system, while others follow consensus, majority or qualified-majority rule. In terms of procedures, some organizations allow for considerable stakeholder input, while others restrict input to a small group of technocratic actors. Likewise, there are a wide variety of possible arrangements at the domestic level. Regulatory oversight may be fragmented across several agencies or unified under one body. Formal procedures and informal processes may include active stakeholder input or may follow a more arms-length model of oversight. The two levels of varying institutional arrangements generate a wide range of possible domestic-international combinations. According to the institutional complementarities logic, some combinations are more likely than others to give the respective domestic regulators influence over international rule-making.

Mattli and Büthe (2003) found, for example, that the decentralized regulatory process within the US for developing product standards, compared to the more hierarchical structure in the EU, put the US at a disadvantage globally at the International Standards Organization (ISO). The US domestic regulatory structure produced several, competing standard setters that owing to ISO rules, which rely on national representatives, left several voices on the sidelines of negotiations. Moreover, the ISO structure incentivized some US representatives to guard information and keep it from competitive US standard setters. By contrast, the European multi-level governance process organized a hierarchy among EU standard setters, creating an efficient flow of information between national firms and their standard setters.

The case of first-mover offers perhaps the most robust case for EU influence based on agenda setting authority. When the regulatory area is densely institutionalized at the international level and the EU is on the right side of a capacity gap, it is well positioned to make its rules the transnational focal point. In contrast to the more diffuse and market-based mechanism of regulatory export, first-mover advantages are triggered by thick institutionalization at the global level, which catalyzes and amplifies disparities in regulatory capacity.

Mutual recognition

In those regulatory domains, which are lightly institutionalized and characterized by relative parity between the regulatory capacity of the two major jurisdictions, the EU is likely to find itself in a much weaker position to influence the behavior of the other power and thus to shape global standards created by transnational bodies. In this context, market actors face conflicting rules of the two most important regulators, both of which are equally capable of exerting their jurisdictional authority. Yet, if the regulators insist on extending their respective standards to govern the firms based in the other's jurisdiction, they invite retaliation. In such settings, powerful regulators might make a show of extending their standards or establishing first-mover advantages. Yet doing so is likely to be a mere effort to improve bargaining position, as regulators anticipate the potential for tit-for-tat downward spirals and thus failure of such unilateralist strategies. In short, parity in regulatory capacity weakens the effect of reversion point tactics. Instead, regulators are likely to pursue a more defensive strategy, in which they attempt to preserve domestic standards at home but do not directly challenge the standards of the other major economic actor. With both jurisdictions making similar calculations, the outcome is likely to be negotiated mutual recognition, a form of sovereignty sharing (Farrell 2003; Nicolaidis and Shaffer 2005). That is, the two powerful jurisdictions would allow market access by the other's firms, so long as each accepted that the other's regime met a negotiated minimum set of standards, said by each to be equivalent of their own. Typically, then, under these conditions, the jurisdictions retain discretion to determine equivalency. That said, such agreements become more difficult to conclude the greater the difference in substantive norms that animate domestic regulatory regimes.

The case of accounting standards is a prominent example in US–EU relations. For much of the post-war period, foreign firms interested in listing on US markets had to reconcile their financial accounts to US Generally Accepted Accounting Principles (USGAAP). For many European firms listed on US markets, this meant that they had to absorb the extra costs of what amounted to reporting in two different formats, a European national standard and the US one. And this duplicative reporting could have profound consequences for the way investors and others interpreted their market capitalization, among other aspects of their financial condition.

European national and EU officials had pressed, in vein, for US recognition of domestic and international accounting standards – without reconciliation. The US finally agreed in 2007, a decision that created a *de facto* mutual recognition regime. The Security and Exchange Commission (SEC) only agreed to allow foreign firms to report in accordance with international accounting standards after the EU required all publically listed companies to use International Financial Reporting Standards (IFRS) and developed relatively equal capacities (to those of the US) to require foreign firms raising capital in the EU to meet equivalence tests. It is true that, in building new capacities, the EU adopted

THE EUROPEAN UNION AS A GLOBAL REGULATOR?

IFRS and thereby increased the salience of the international accounting institutions. Yet it is also clear that the US accommodation and thus the mutual recognition regime was more a reflection of the new parity in regulatory capacities than a changed view of international accounting institutions (Posner 2010). If the latter were the case, SEC officials would have allowed US, not just foreign, companies to adopt IFRS, and they would have accepted mutual recognition sooner, perhaps in 2002, when the EU adopted IFRS, rather than in 2007, shortly after the EU introduced the legal provisions to require an equivalence determination before US firms using USGAAP could raise capital in Europe. The case thus illustrates how relative parity in regulatory capacities, under conditions of light international institutionalization, encourage great powers to forge mutual recognition arrangements.

While mutual recognition agreements offer an elegant solution to regulatory conflict between the major regulatory players, they have proven elusive in most areas – suggesting that an additional variable, such as a shared normative framework, might be necessary for the successful negotiation of mutual recognition regimes (Nicolaidis and Shaffer 2005). If each side retains discretion to determine equivalent foreign regulations, firms from jurisdictions with the more stringent rules will fear an unfair playing field and their regulators will thus be hesitant to enter mutual recognition regimes. The sluggish progress toward reaching a Transatlantic Trade and Investment Partnership, for instance, shows the potential limits of such a strategy. This is in part due to stakeholders who are unwilling to allow equal market access to foreign market players; but it is also owing to the significant differences in regulatory preferences and approaches. The interaction of parity in regulatory capacity and the relatively weak institutionalization could very well incentivize the creation of rival rules instead of the kind of sovereignty sharing necessary for extensive co-operation (Drezner 2007).

Coalition-building

Finally, in domains characterized by parity in regulatory capacity, powerful jurisdictions may use densely institutionalized arenas to advance their interests through strategies more frequently associated with domestic political arenas. As in the first-mover strategy, regulators hope to leverage international institutions to lock-in transnational standards that reflect their interests. In contrast to the first-mover quadrant, however, regulatory powers are not able to shape the agenda by using their asymmetrical regulatory capacity to out maneuver other great powers. Instead, in this context – approaching what we might call a rule-based 'global politics' – the coalitional dynamics to arise more closely resemble domestic regulatory contests as the EU and other participants play by the rules of international institutions (Alter 2014; Davis 2004; Kissack 2015; Risse-Kappen 1995; Sabel and Zeitlin 2010; Tarrow 2001).

Coalition-building in international institutions can be quite complex, involving a host of different negotiating parties – public and private – behaving in accordance with the different rules of different organizations (Jupille 1999; Meunier 2005). The EU will be best positioned to influence global standards when it can build a winning coalition of supporters behind its rules and block the rules of an alternative coalition supported by other regulatory great powers. Depending on the decision-rules of the rule-making body, EU success, then, depends to an important extent on the differences in its preferences from those of other decision-makers in the organization. In those cases where the EU is a preference outlier, it will have little power. In those cases, however, where the EU can forge a bloc of like-minded partners, either through linkage strategies or deliberative approaches, it will be able to use the organization to promote its rules. Alasdair Young (2014), for example, demonstrates this argument in food and safety standards developed through the Codex Alimentarius, where EU preference extremes stymie its efforts to change global standards. And in those cases where the EU builds a change coalition, the outcome is not always identical with EU internal rules. In short, such coalition building requires compromise. Similarly, Meunier (2005) has argued that the EU is best positioned to influence global trade negotiations when it supports a *status quo* position as the EU needs few partners to block negotiation progress.

In contrast to the mutual recognition quadrant, in which the EU has little capacity to shape global rules, the coalition-building quadrant demonstrates the powerful role that institutions play. Yet in order to overcome the *status quo*, the EU must find a significant number of regulatory allies. In those cases, however, the EU may not find support for the simple extension of EU rules.

CONCLUSION

This contribution attempts to better define the boundary conditions of EU influence by focusing on how EU power is channeled through particular policy strategies, which themselves are conditioned on the broader global regulatory context. Using two key dimensions of this context – relative regulatory capacity and institutional density – we derive an analytic typology of EU policy strategies.

For reasons of theory, clarity and space constraints, the framework focuses on institutional dimensions of the global regulatory context and thus holds many other related factors constant. As a simplifying assumption, we consider cases where there is significant distributional conflict centered on clashing regulatory practices. Future work will thus want to examine the ways in which the global context shapes normative alignment (Newman and Posner 2015). A strong ideational frame such as 'the Washington Consensus' or neoliberal principle may become part of the global regulatory context and as a result shape EU influence (Abdelal 2007). We would expect that in cases of strong normative consensus, the EU may either play a relatively inconsequential role as one of many regulatory followers or as part of the leading coalition among like-minded regulators. In either case, we would expect the context to be a strong determinant of the result, as there would be less space for political contestation.

Despite these limitations, we believe the framework improves on current understanding of global regulation and the EU's role in developing it. In keeping with the 'new interdependence' approach of Farrell and Newman (2014), the contribution emphasizes the global consequences of the relative distribution of domestic institutions. Rather than depict domestic institutions as simple veto points that filter and aggregate domestic preferences, or as sources of national capacities for individual states, the framework suggests why scholars should treat them as important elements of the global systemic context.

Specifically, our approach helps to understand competing empirical claims, discussed above, about EU influence and impotence and sharpens the logic behind theoretical propositions. Our argument makes clear that power resources alone do not correspond directly to outcomes. Rather, such resources must be filtered through global policy strategies that serve as the means to achieve particular goals. Empirically, the four types of strategies in Figure 1 lay out in sharp relief why scholars can arrive at radically different conclusions: the EU is likely to adopt different strategies under different configurations of the global regulatory context. Accordingly, EU power resources are expected to be less effective when conditions give rise to coalition-building strategies, as in the case of food and safety standards developed through the Codex Alimentarius, than when the context pushes the EU toward first-mover agenda-setting strategies, as in the case of standards development in the International Standards Organization. Likewise, the outcomes in bilateral EU–US negotiations over financial services regulation, where the EU has operated largely under a mutual recognition strategy, will differ from those in disputes over chemical regulations, where the EU has adopted regulatory export strategies. The approach thus integrates a number of empirical claims that have either been depicted as competing arguments or have largely ignored one another.

Theoretically, using our framework, the sometimes-wide divide between civilian and normative power approaches becomes a secondary issue. Regulation is based both on the substance of rules and the institutions that enforce them. Thus, the concept of relative regulatory capacity subsumes and integrates elements of both types of power. Moreover, our approach underscores that the embeddedness of normative and civilian power within a particular regulatory context emerges as the primary determinant of EU foreign regulatory engagement. In this sense, the analytic framework reorients the theoretical debate away from an artificial distinction between norms and markets and contextualizes an array of causal processes within the broader global environment. Put another way, EU power resources (regardless of their particular attributes) must be situated both in terms of their relationship to the power resources of other great powers, as well as to the institutions in which great powers interact. In so doing, the framework suggests the policy strategies available to the EU (as well as other regulatory great powers) and better estimates the likelihood of EU effectiveness in global regulatory debates.

THE EUROPEAN UNION AS A GLOBAL REGULATOR?

Biographical notes: Abraham L. Newman is an associate professor at the BMW Center for German and European Studies in the Edmund A. Walsh School of Foreign Service at Georgetown University, Washington DC. Elliot Posner is an associate professor of political science at Case Western Reserve University, Cleveland.

ACKNOWLEDGEMENTS

Drafts of this contribution were presented at the 'Regulatory power Europe? Assessing the EU's efforts to shape global rules' Jean Monnet Chair Workshop, Georgia Institute of Technology, Atlanta, 18 April 2014, and at the 14th Biennial International Conference of the European Union Studies Association, Boston, 5 March 2015. We thank Darius Ornston, Sofia Perez, the other participants of these events and, especially, Alasdair Young, as well as two anonymous referees.

REFERENCES

Abbott, K. and Snidal, D. (2000). 'Hard and soft law in international governance', *International Organization* 54: 421–56.

Abdelal, R. (2007) *Capital Rules: The Construction of Global Finance*, Cambridge: Cambridge University Press.

Alter, K. (2014) *The New Terrain of International Law: Courts, Politics, Rights*, Princeton, NJ: Princeton University Press.

Andonova, L.B. (2004) *Transnational Politics of the Environment: The European Union and Environmental Policy in Central and Eastern Europe*, Cambridge, MA: MIT Press.

Axelrod, R. and Keohane, R.O. (1985) 'Achieving cooperation under anarchy: strategies and institutions', *World Politics* 38(01): 226–54.

Bach, D. and Newman, A.L. (2007) 'The European regulatory state and global public policy: micro-institutions and macro-influence', *Journal of European Public Policy* 16(4): 827–46.

Bach, D. and Newman, A.L. (2010) 'Governing lipitor and lipstick: capacity, sequencing, and power in international pharmaceutical and cosmetics regulation', *Review of International Political Economy* 17(4): 665–95.

Bicchi, F. (2006) '"Our size fits all": normative power Europe and the Mediterranean', *Journal of European Public Policy* 13(2): 286–303.

Birchfield, V.L. (2015) 'Coercion with kid gloves: the European Union's role in shaping a global regulatory framework for aviation emissions', *Journal of European Public Policy*, doi: 10.1080/13501763.2015.1046904.

Bradford, A. (2012) 'The Brussels effect', *Northwestern University Law Review* 107: 1.

Bretherton, C. and Vogler, J. (1999) *The European Union as a Global Actor*, London: Routledge.

THE EUROPEAN UNION AS A GLOBAL REGULATOR?

Bretherton, C. and Vogler, J. (2013) 'A global actor past its peak?', *International Relations* 27(3): 375–90.

de Búrca, G. (2013) 'EU external relations: the governance mode of foreign policy', in Bart Van Vooren, Steven Blockmans and Jan Wouters (eds), *The Legal Dimension of Global Governance: What Role for the EU*, Oxford: Oxford Univeristy Press, pp. 39–58.

Büthe, T. and Mattli, W. (2011) *The New Global Rulers: The Privatization of Regulation in the World Economy*, Princeton, NJ: Princeton University Press.

Copelovitch, M.S. and Putnam, T.L. (2014) 'Design in context: existing international agreements and new cooperation', *International Organization* 68(02): 471–93.

Damro, C. (2012) 'Market power Europe', *Journal of European Public Policy* 19(5): 682–99.

Damro, C. (2015) 'Market power Europe: exploring a dynamic conceptual framework', *Journal of European Public Policy*, doi: 10.1080/13501763.2015.1046903.

Davis, C.L. (2004). 'International institutions and issue linkage: building support for agricultural trade liberalization', *The American Political Science Review* 98(1): 153–69.

Drezner, D. (2007). *All Politics Is Global: Explaining International Regulatory Regimes*, Princeton, NJ: Princeton University Press.

Falkner, R. (2007) 'The political economy of "normative power" Europe: EU environmental leadership in international biotechnology regulation', *Journal of European Public Policy* 14(4): 507–26.

Falleti, T.G. and Lynch, J.F. (2009) 'Context and causal mechanisms in political analysis', *Comparative Political Studies* 42(9): 1143–66.

Farrell, H. (2003) 'Constructing the international foundations of e-commerce: the EU–US safe harbor arrangement', *International Organization* 2: 277–306.

Farrell, H. and Newman, A.L. (2010) 'Making global markets: historical institutionalism in international political economy', *Review of International Political Economy* 17(4): 609–38.

Farrell, H. and Newman, A.L. (2014) 'Domestic institutions beyond the nation-state: charting the new interdependence approach', *World Politics* 66(02): 331–63.

Finnemore, M. (1996) *National Interests in International Society*, Ithaca, NY: Cornell University Press.

Frieden, J. (1999) 'Actors and preferences in international relations', in D. Lake and R. Powell (eds), *Strategic Choice and International Relations*, Princeton, NJ: Princeton University Press, pp. 39–76.

George, A. and Bennett, A. (2005) *Case Studies and Theory Development in the Social Sciences*, Cambridge, MA: MIT Press.

Green, J.F. (2014) *Rethinking Private Authority: Agents and Entrepreneurs in Global Environmental Governance*, Princeton, NJ: Princeton University Press.

Gruber, L. (2000) *Ruling the World: Power Politics and the Rise of Supranational Institutions*, Princeton, NJ: Princeton University Press.

Jacoby, W. and Meunier, S. (2010) 'Europe and the management of globalization', *Journal of European Public Policy* 17(3): 299–317.

James, S. and Lake, D. (1989) 'The second face of hegemony: Britain's repeal of the Corn Laws and the American Walker Tariff of 1846', *International Organization* 43(1): 1–29.

Jervis, R. (1997) *System Effects: Complexity in Political and Social Life*, Princeton, NJ: Princenton University Press.

Jordana, J. and Levi-Faur, D. (2004) *The Politics of Regulation: Institutions and Regulatory Reform for the Age of Governance*, Northhampton: Edward Elgar.

Jupille, J. (1999) 'The European Union and international outcomes', *International Organization* 53(2): 409–21.

THE EUROPEAN UNION AS A GLOBAL REGULATOR?

Kelemen, R.D. and Vogel, D. (2010) 'Trading places: the role of the United States and the European Union in international environmental politics', *Comparative Political Studies* 43(4): 427–56.

Keohane, R. (1984) *After Hegemony*, Princeton, NJ: Princeton University Press.

Kissack, R. (2015) '"Man overboard!" Was EU influence on the Maritime Labour Convention lost at sea?', *Journal of European Public Policy*, doi: 10.1080/13501763.2015.1046899.

Laïdi, Z. (2008) *EU Foreign Policy in a Globalized World: Normative Power and Social Preferences*, New York: Routledge.

Lall, R. (2014) 'Timing as a source of regulatory influence: a technical elite network analysis of global finance', *Regulation & Governance*, doi: 10.1111/rego.12050.

Lavenex, S. and Schimmelfennig, F. (2009) 'EU rules beyond EU Borders: theorizing external governance in European politics', *Journal of European Public Policy* 16(6): 791–812.

Leblond, P. (2011) 'EU, US and international accounting standards: a delicate balancing act in governing global finance', *Journal of European Public Policy* 18(3): 443–61.

Lütz, S. (2011) 'Back to the future? The domestic sources of transatlantic regulation', *Review of International Political Economy* 18(4): iii–xxii.

Manners, I. (2006) 'Normative power Europe reconsidered: beyond the crossroads', *Journal of European Public Policy* 13(2): 182–99.

Mattli, W. and Büthe, T. (2003) 'Setting international standards: technological rationality or primacy of power', *World Politics* 56(1): 1–42.

Mattli, W. and Woods, N. (2009) *The Politics of Global Regulation*, Princeton, NJ: Princeton University Press.

McNamara, K. (2015) *The Politics of Everyday Europe*, Oxford: Oxford University Press.

McNamara, K. and Meunier, S. (2002) 'Between national sovereignty and international power: what external voice for the euro', *International Affairs* 78(4): 849–68.

Meunier, S. (2005) *Trading Voices: The European Union in International Commercial Negotiations*, Princeton, NJ: Princeton University Press.

Müller, P., Kudrna, Z. and Falkner, G. (2014) 'EU–global interactions: policy export, import, promotion and protection', *Journal of European Public Policy* 21(8): 1102–19.

Newman, A. (2008) *Protectors of Privacy: Regulating Personal Data in the Global Economy*, Ithaca, NY: Cornell University Press.

Newman, A. and Posner, E. (2011) 'International interdependence and regulatory power: authority, mobility, and markets', *European Journal of International Relations* 17(4): 589–610.

Newman, A. and Posner, E. (2015) 'Transnational feedbacks, soft law, and preferences in global financial regulation', Paper presented at the 14th Biennial EUSA Conference, Boston, MA, 5–7 March.

Nicolaidis, K. and Shaffer, G. (2005) 'Transnational mutual recognition regimes: governance without global government', *Law and Contemporary Problems* 68: 263.

Oatley, T. (2011) 'The reductionist gamble: open economy politics in the global economy', *International Organization* 65(02): 311–41.

Pollack, M.A. and Shaffer, G.C. (2009) *When Cooperation Fails: The International Law and Politics of Genetically Modified Foods*, New York: Oxford University Press.

Porter, T. (2005) *Globalization and Finance*, Cambridge: Polity.

Posner, E. (2009) 'Making rules for global finance: transatlantic regulatory cooperation at the turn of the millennium', *International Organization* 63(4): 665–99.

Posner, E. (2010) 'Sequence as explanation: the international politics of accounting standards', *Review of International Political Economy* 17(4): 639–64.

Quaglia, L. (2013) 'The European Union, the USA and international standard setting by regulatory fora in finance', *New Political Economy* 19(3): 427–44.

THE EUROPEAN UNION AS A GLOBAL REGULATOR?

Quaglia, L. (2014) *The European Union and Global Financial Regulation*, Oxford: Oxford University Press.

Richards, J. (1999) 'Toward a positive theory of international institutions: regulating international aviation markets', *International Organization* 53(1): 1–37.

Risse-Kappen, T. (1994) 'Ideas do not float freely: transnational coalitions, domestic structures, and the end of the Cold War', *International Organization* 48(02): 185–214.

Risse-Kappen, T. (1995) *Bringing Transnational Actors Back In*, Cambridge: Cambridge University Press.

Ruggie, John Gerard. 1998. *Constructing the World Polity: Essays on International Institutionalization.* Psychology Press.

Sabel, C. and Zeitlin, J. (2010) *Experimentalist Governance in the European Union: Towards a New Architecutre*, Oxford: Oxford University Press.

Sbragia, A. (2010) 'The EU, the US, and trade policy: competitive interdependence in the management of globalization', *Journal of European Public Policy* 17(3): 368–82.

Simmons, B. (2001) 'The international politics of harmonization: the case of capital market regulation', *International Organization* 55: 589–620.

Slaughter, A.-M. (2004) *A New World Order*, Princeton, NJ: Princeton University Press.

Tarrow, S. (2001) 'Transnational politics: contention and institutions in international politics', *Annual Review of Political Science* 4(1): 1–20.

Vogel, D. (1995). *Trading Up: Consumer and Environmental Regulation in a Global Economy*, Cambridge, MA: Harvard University Press.

Vogel, D. (2012) *The Politics of Precaution: Regulating Health, Safety, and Environmental Risks in Europe and the United States*, Princeton, NJ: Princeton University Press.

Waltz, K. (1979) *Theory of International Politics*, Reading, MA: Addison-Wesley.

Weber, S. (1994) 'The origins of the European Bank of Reconstruction', *International Organization* 48: 1–38.

Wendt, A. (1998) 'On constitution and causation in international relations', *Review of International Studies* 24(05): 101–18.

Young, A.R. (2003) 'Political transfer and "trading up"? Transatlantic trade in genetically modified food and US politics', *World Politics* 55(July): 457–84.

Young, A.R. (2014) 'Europe as a global regulator? The limits of EU influence in international food safety standards', *Journal of European Public Policy* 21(6): 904–22.

Young, A.R. (2015a) 'The European Union as a Global Regulator? Context and Comparison', *Journal of European Public Policy*, doi: 10.1080/13501763.2015.1046902.

Young, A.R. (2015b) 'Liberalizing trade, not exporting rules: the limits to regulatory coordination in the EU's "new generation" preferential trade agreements', *Journal of European Public Policy*, doi: 10.1080/13501763.2015.1046900.

THE EUROPEAN UNION AS A GLOBAL REGULATOR?

The MPE conceptualization also serves as a call to the EU-as-a-power debates to consider more fully the findings of CIPE research, including the types of empirical research undertaken in this collection. While the following discussion takes note of and draws from the other contributions, it is not intended to serve as a conclusion that summarizes and synthesizes the collective findings. But given the prominent role of regulation and regulatory processes for MPE, this collection provides a particularly useful context for undertaking a stock-taking exercise of the conceptualization.

Contributions to the EU-as-a-power debates have helped to establish that the EU should be taken seriously as an international actor. These debates may be fragmented today, but they remain valuable efforts to address the ever-present ontological questions about the EU's existence and seek to provide conceptual bases from which to understand the EU in international affairs. The aim of this contribution is not to provide the definitive statement on which conceptualization of the EU as a power is best. Rather, as a stock-taking exercise, the contribution aims to clarify and elaborate important aspects of MPE and to explore the utility of employing it as a *conceptual framework* – not an explanatory theory – that provides a rethink of and a way to take forward the debates.

As a conceptual framework, the contribution finds that MPE can serve as a basis for identifying and organizing the factors and concepts that inform empirical research and help to drive the development of explanatory theory. When MPE is viewed and employed as such an analytical tool, the contribution also finds that it is dynamic in the sense of being flexible enough to allow and encourage testing of various explanatory factors and to incorporate insights and new findings from the growing scholarly work on EU external relations. The dynamic nature of the framework also helps to generate analytical advantages through empirical and methodological contributions that further our understanding of the EU as an international regulator and, more generally, as a power.

The contribution proceeds in the following manner. The next section identifies general contours of the EU-as-a-power debates, which help to inform the subsequent identification and discussion of areas in which MPE may make contributions. The contribution then elaborates MPE as a conceptual framework and discusses the nature and utility of such an analytical tool. Next, the contribution turns to recent research that helps to expand two important components of the framework – the three core characteristics of MPE and the exercise of power through externalization. The following section reflects upon further areas in which MPE may generate analytical advantages for the EU-as-a-power debates. The contribution concludes with a summary of the findings and their implications for future research.

CONTOURS OF THE EU-AS-A-POWER DEBATES

The study of the EU in international politics started with and, in many ways, continues to be a reaction to the reluctance of state-centric International Relations (IR) scholarship to problematize the EU as an actor in and of itself

(Bretherton and Vogler 2005; Niemann and Bretherton 2013; Rosamond 2005). This need to situate the EU and its apparent uniqueness as an actor has helped to generate a proliferation of conceptualizations of the EU as a power in the international system. The resulting 'EU-as-a–power' debates (Damro 2012) identify particular characteristics that may contribute to the EU as a power and prioritize questions about what kind of power the EU is, what the EU says as a power and what the EU does as a power.

Starting with civilian power, Duchêne (1972) suggested that the EU's unique characteristics made it a different kind of actor for which military power had been supplanted by civilian power.[2] Since Duchêne's rather 'imprecise description' (Orbie 2008: 5), the array of particular characteristics and labels for understanding the EU as a power have grown considerably. But this proliferation has left the debates rather fragmented among different conceptualizations that are often characterized as rivals. In this sense, the various contributions can be thought of as resembling 'debates', more so than a coherent research programme of scholarly inquiry.[3] As a result, the debates may have missed opportunities to advance our more general understandings of the EU as a global actor.

Attempting to generalize about the EU-as-a-power debates is a risky business because of the rich diversity of the various contributions and conceptualizations. But there are contours that can be identified for the debates in general, if not specifically applicable to all of the contributions. While general, these contours help to identify empirical and analytical challenges that serve to inform the subsequent reflections on MPE.

Although an understanding of the EU as *sui generis* is (at least implicitly) common in the extant literature (Phelan 2012: 367), it creates the so-called 'N = 1 problem' that undermines the ability to generalize about and from the EU's dynamics and to engage with other scholarly literatures.[4] This has led to an enduring problem for the EU-as-a-power debates: the perceived N = 1 treatment of the EU as *sui generis* can keep the research rather isolated and self-referential, effectively discouraging interaction with other more generalizable literatures. As Phelan argues, 'the study of the EU is not well integrated into – indeed, it appears increasingly segregated from – wider international relations scholarship' (2012: 368). As a result of the N = 1 limitation and a tendency to rely on Duchêne's (1972) original but imprecise description of civilian power as a 'conceptual anchor' (Nicolaïdis and Howse 2003: 344), the EU-as–a-power debates have a tendency to be viewed as largely descriptive and often contributing little to the development of explanatory theory. Forsberg (2011) even goes so far as to argue that prominent conceptualizations in the debates resemble ideal types in need of further clarification in order to overcome their lack of explanatory power.[5]

A *sui generis* focus on the EU can also limit full consideration of the analytical concept of power itself and the way it works. To overcome such a shortcoming, contributions to the debates have usefully employed insights, to varying degrees, from Barnett and Duvall's (2005) IR taxonomy of power (Bicchi 2006; Diez *et al.* 2006; Holden 2009; Lavenex 2014).[6] But the general contour of the

THE EUROPEAN UNION AS A GLOBAL REGULATOR?

debates is an absence of investigations into the fungibility of power across various policy areas.[7] In other words, the debates do not undertake concerted efforts to determine the extent to which power in one policy area can become power in other areas. Likewise, disagreement and analytical confusion can arise over exactly what the EU as a power is trying to promote in different policy areas. For example, from a civilian power perspective, the EU may be exercising power to promote civilian ends. However, it is often ambiguous or unclear exactly what those ends or objectives are, especially when they appear inconsistent or are inconsistently pursued in practice across different policy areas (Smith 2005).

Finally, when the EU-as-a-power debates do explore causality, there is often a tendency to view material/interest-based and social/ideational factors as competing sources of power. Moreover, while there are material/interest-based critiques and studies of the EU as a power (Hyde-Price 2006; Pollack 2012; Zimmerman 2007), the debates tend to be dominated by accounts that privilege the social and ideational sources of power. As Youngs (2004: 415) argues, 'Many – probably, most – analysts have come to posit a pre-eminence of ideational dynamics as key to the EU's distinctiveness as an international actor.' Owing to this analytical focus, the debates risk overlooking the complex interplay of material *and* social factors that contribute to the EU's identity and exercise of power across policy areas.[8] This leads to a tendency to emphasize the persuasive nature and tools of the EU's exercise of power and a failure to make explicit the potential role played by various causal factors that may arise from the EU's market size, institutional features and domestic interest contestation in its exercise of power.

MPE AND THE UTILITY OF CONCEPTUAL FRAMEWORKS

The MPE conceptualization is not merely another critique of the previous contributions to the EU-as-a-power debates. Rather, drawing from the CIPE literature on the EU as a regulator, it serves as an acknowledgement and response to the more general contours of the debates outlined above. As such, MPE can be thought of as a way to engage with existing critiques and to develop an explicit and clear *conceptual framework* that may help to move forward the debates.

The EU's identity – from where the MPE conceptualization begins – is based upon three inter-related and mutually reinforcing characteristics: market size; institutional features; and interest contestation. Through this formulation, MPE does not depend upon the EU being a *sui generis* actor. Rather, the three characteristics are drawn from the general CIPE literature and may be common to any market power's identity (Damro 2012; 686–9). While the CIPE literature usefully identifies important and relevant causal relationships among factors that may be associated with these three characteristics, it is important to highlight that the original formulation of MPE is not, in and of itself, an explanatory theory that posits causal relationships. It may, however, add value to such pursuits when employed as a conceptual framework for theorizing about such relationships.

Conceptual frameworks, although not always made explicit, are essential components of empirical research processes and projects that help to direct and ground researchers (Ravitch and Riggan 2012). While there is no single definition of 'conceptual frameworks', they may generally be understood as abstract representations or analytical tools that help make conceptual distinctions and organize ideas, thereby bringing structure and coherence to empirical research. As part of a research process, conceptual frameworks are also dynamic in the sense that they are flexible and open to revision and expansion as new findings emerge from ongoing scholarly inquiry. A conceptual framework is, therefore, a tool for and a necessary step in researching and understanding social, economic and political phenomena. The phenomena in question for MPE are the EU's identity and nature as a power and its exercise of power via the externalization of market-related policies and regulatory measures.

As Ravitch and Riggan (2012) argue, researchers often fail to make clear distinctions between terms like conceptual frameworks and theory or theoretical frameworks. While the terms should not be conflated, conceptual frameworks do relate to theory and may contribute to theory testing and development. For example, Blaikie (2000: 144) argues that conceptual frameworks 'lend themselves to the development of propositions about relationships between concepts, and are intended to apply to a wide range of situations'.[5] For MPE, the 'concepts' among which propositions about relationships may be developed are drawn from the three characteristics and the phenomenon of externalization. The 'wide range of situations' may be thought of as varying across time, geographic location and policy area. In this sense, while a conceptual framework is 'broader than traditional notions of theory' (Shields and Rangarajan 2013: 24), explanatory theories can be seen as 'sub-components' that may address certain aspects of the conceptual framework (Ravitch and Riggan 2012).

MPE can be viewed as an explicit conceptual framework that distinguishes among three distinct characteristics of the EU's identity and the EU's exercise of power via externalization. Such ideas are not simple. But elaborating, organizing and making them explicit in a conceptual framework is an important step in establishing them as analytical tools for advancing our understanding of the EU as a power. In the MPE context, 'sub-component' theories of the conceptual framework may be seen as explanatory theories that identify relevant causal relationships between and among the three core characteristics and externalization. At the same time, such sub-component theories may help to identify additional factors, such as external factors, that can help to expand the dynamic MPE conceptual framework. These sub-component theories are numerous and may include, for example, CIPE contributions that help to generate explanations (for the EU and other actors) of the causes of externalization. As will be discussed, empirical contributions to this collection and the scholarly works referred to below may be seen as representative of such sub-component theories.

THE EUROPEAN UNION AS A GLOBAL REGULATOR?

Among sub-component theories, material/interest-based and social/ideational explanations and causal mechanisms may be identified and associated with the three characteristics and externalization of MPE. But as a conceptual framework, MPE remains flexible and does not simply organize the characteristics as competing explanations for externalization. Rather, the proposition that the three core characteristics are inter-related and mutually reinforcing encourages us to think about the conceptual *and/or* causal connections and relationships among them in order to generate more complete understandings of the EU's identity and actions as a power. By not privileging or necessarily excluding *a priori* any one type of causal factor, MPE allows us to see potential connections and provides a broader basis from which, ultimately, to theorize and conduct empirical research that can evaluate causality in the analysis of the EU as a power. Such engagement with different causal factors and mechanisms may even be seen as 'healthy' and may 'help scholars move away from perpetual rivalry in disciplinary "ism" wars and toward dialogue across theoretical perspectives' (Barnett and Duvall 2005: 45).

In short, conceptual frameworks operate as important analytical tools that help to advance knowledge by organizing empirical research and grounding theory testing and development while also remaining open to adjustment and revision. Owing to the fragmentation and often descriptive nature of the EU-as-a-power debates, such a dynamic analytical tool that remains open to consideration of various potential causal factors and mechanisms provides an opportunity to build our understanding of the EU as a power and both complements and contributes to research aimed at explaining the EU as a power.

NEW RESEARCH FINDINGS AND MPE

While MPE in its original formulation did not specify causal relationships among the three core characteristics and externalization, the characteristics can help to identify factors and concepts that may be operationalized as independent variables with the potential to condition externalization. In a similar manner, the conceptual framework can benefit from new research findings that emerge from the testing of sub-component theories designed to engage more readily with the causes of externalization. This section examines such new findings that are emerging from research that has engaged in different ways with the framework.

Three characteristics of MPE

The greatest attention in the recent research has been related to the first characteristic of market size.[10] Perhaps this is not surprising, given the label of *market power Europe*. But privileging the term 'market' in the label MPE does not mean that the other characteristics of institutional features and interest contestation are analytically less important than market size. It is simply an indication that the EU's identity, both historically and presently, rests crucially upon market integration, an ongoing experiment in social, economic and political organization that intimately involves and deeply implicates the EU's various institutional features and actors as well as interest groups alignments. While market size is an important characteristic of the EU's identity, the extent to which it matters as an individual causal factor varies considerably. The recent studies that grapple with this characteristic tend to suggest that, while market size may be necessary for the EU to be a power, by itself this characteristic is not typically sufficient to explain the EU as a power.[11] This finding encourages further scrutiny of the other two core characteristic and the extent to which they and market size are inter-related and mutually reinforcing.

The second characteristic of institutional features is broadly formulated and sufficiently flexible to cover a wide variety of aspects and actors that may be seen as fitting into an understanding of the EU as a regulatory state (Majone 1994, 1997).[12] If the EU is a regulatory state, MPE must take into consideration the policy-making processes and decision-making rules for issuing regulatory measures, which can vary depending on the policy area in question. But while the EU's institutional rules are important, this characteristic does not neglect the role of actors. For example, MPE must also consider a variety of actors that operate within these processes and rules and that may condition externalization, including EU member states and institutions – e.g., European Commission, European Parliament, Council of Ministers, European Court of Justice.

Owing to the regulatory focus of the conceptualization, MPE also considers the various networks of national regulators and EU-level regulatory agencies that may condition externalization. Herein arises the focus in the conceptual framework on the EU's institutional ability, or regulatory capacity (Bach and Newman 2007; Bradford 2014; Young 2015), to externalize its market-related policies and regulatory measures. But MPE is not limited to regulatory capacity. Rather, the dynamism of the framework allows this second characteristic to be open to a wide array of possible actors, institutions and network or governance arrangements that may play a role in the development and externalization of EU market-related policies and regulatory measures. For example, the framework can benefit from identification and consideration of the actors and institutional mechanisms (such as peer review) that are now often involved in what has been termed rule-making by 'experimentalist governance' (Sabel and Zeitlin 2010). Such rule-making includes a number of new tools that may be usefully considered in the context of the MPE framework. In particular, when the mechanisms of experimentalist governance extend and develop on a transnational or global scale (Zeitlin 2015), they may contribute to the potential for the EU to externalize its internal market-related policies and regulatory measures.[13]

Recent research that has engaged more directly with the MPE conceptualization has also identified a variety of institutional features that may help to condition the EU's externalization, including domestic regulatory templates (Quaglia 2014b), institutional rules and internal cohesiveness (da Conceição-

THE EUROPEAN UNION AS A GLOBAL REGULATOR?

Heldt and Meunier 2014), EU competence and the type of international agreement being negotiated (Jurje and Lavenex 2014) and the stringency of EU standards (Young 2014). In sum, these institutional features fit well with the MPE framework and help to expand the potential factors that may condition the relationship between the second core characteristic and externalization.

The final core characteristic of MPE, interest contestation, can also be formulated in a broad sense and understood generally as societal pressure. This characteristic, therefore, encourages consideration of the potential pressure exerted by all types of interest groups, not simply firms or economic actors. The preferences of such domestic actors may also vary depending on the type of regulation in question.[14] The ways in which these various societal actors contest their preferences and the extent to which they form pro-externalization coalitions capable of influencing decision-makers should help us to understand the extent to which the EU seeks to externalize its market-related policies and regulatory measures. For example, European airlines *and* environmental groups have been found to pressure the EU for externalization of aircraft emissions standards (Staniland 2012). But the influence of such societal pressure need not be limited to actors within the EU because civil society actors in EU partner countries have also been found to condition externalization (Postnikov and Bastiaens 2014). Finally, societal pressure may also be linked to the other two core characteristics because, while market power may incentivize some groups to push for externalization, they need appropriate institutional channels through which to lobby for their preferences (Turkina and Postnikov 2014).

MPE's dynamism also allows adjustments to take into account new findings that identify additional factors not directly linked to any one of the three characteristics. For example, despite its analytical starting point (the EU's identity), the conceptual framework can accommodate and build upon findings related to concepts like the EU's actorness and its effectiveness (Niemann and Bretherton 2013). Similarly, the EU's exercise of power may be conditioned by external or international contextual factors, including the constellation of preferences and distribution of power (Young 2014), geographical proximity and perceived push factors from third countries (Jurje and Lavenex 2014) and competing mandates of international organizations (Staniland 2012). In addition, Newman and Posner (2015) argue for the importance of the global regulatory context. Given their potential importance, MPE analyses need to create room for consideration of such factors, especially the ways in which they influence the actors involved in externalization and the ways in which they are transmitted through the three characteristics of MPE. Indeed, the original formulation of MPE warned of the importance of considering such 'external pressures' in the analysis of externalization (Damro 2012: 690). The role of such factors in understanding the EU as a power should, therefore, be considered in tandem with the largely domestic factors arising from the three characteristics of the conceptual framework.

THE EUROPEAN UNION AS A GLOBAL REGULATOR?

Externalization

As Young (2014) notes, various terms have been employed in the literature to capture what MPE refers to as 'externalization'.[15] For MPE, externalization:

> occurs when the institutions and actors of the EU attempt to get other actors to adhere to a level of regulation similar to that in effect in the European single market or to behave in a way that generally satisfies or conforms to the EU's market-related policies and regulatory measures. (Damro 2012: 690)

This is not a particularly high standard in the sense that it does not require the EU to attempt to get other actors to take on board verbatim all the technical details of European policies and regulations. In fact, getting other actors to behave in a way that *generally satisfies or conforms to* European rules may include the EU externalizing rules that are not identical to its own (see below). It does, however, capture a phenomenon through which the EU may exercise power on potentially all other types of public and private actors in the international system.

Through an MPE approach, externalization can be understood and explored in two stages: the study of EU attempts (or non-attempts) to externalize and the study of actual success or influence via externalization. In the first stage, the factors that contribute to the likelihood of attempts at externalization are analysed, such as the significance of market size, the effect of institutional features and the formation of and contestation between pro- and anti-externalization coalitions (Damro 2012). In conceptual terms, this is a fairly straightforward understanding of externalization: the EU intentionally undertakes an effort to get other actors to adhere to or behave in a way that generally satisfies its market-related policies and regulatory measures.

There are, however, other possibilities for externalization that are worth exploring in the first stage. For example, the EU may intentionally decide for any number of reasons not to undertake an attempt at externalization.[16] But even in instances of such an apparent non-attempt, it is possible that the EU may still externalize unintentionally (Bradford 2012; Vogel 1995). Given the EU's 'presence' (Allen and Smith 1990; Damro 2012) and the potentially inadvertent pressures that follow from the three characteristics of MPE, unintentionality remains an important element of EU externalization and, therefore, needs to be considered an essential component of the conceptualization.

Cases of unintentional externalization via a non-attempt may be rare and methodologically difficult to identify, but they may resemble the mechanisms of policy convergence that Holzinger and Knill (2005) refer to as transnational communication: lesson-drawing; transnational problem-solving; emulation; and international policy promotion.[17] While these four mechanisms require some degree of communication between the EU and other actors, that communication from the European side does not necessarily have to be motivated by an explicit intent to get the other actor to adhere to or behave in conformity

THE EUROPEAN UNION AS A GLOBAL REGULATOR?

with the EU's market-related policies and regulatory measures. Rather, the communication may simply comprise the sharing of information that, at least theoretically, can be absent an intent to externalize.[18] If so, a case would exist in which the EU did not attempt to externalize, but an 'unintentional tool' was exercised that may contribute to the success of externalization in the second stage.

The second stage of externalization is where much of the CIPE literature and empirical contributions to this collection (Birchfield 2015; Kissack 2015; Young 2015) focus their analyses to ascertain the extent of EU influence. As Young (2014) notes, much of the literature on the EU as a global regulator tends to treat the EU as a dominant player. While MPE draws from this literature to emphasize the importance of looking at the EU as a regulatory actor, it leaves claims about the extent to which the EU is indeed a dominant global regulator to second-stage empirical testing. Just because the EU can be understood as MPE and may be analysed as MPE does not mean that it always gets – whether intentionally or unintentionally – other actors to adhere to or behave in a way that generally satisfies its market-related policies and regulatory measures. Failure is a very real possibility. What can be said from an MPE perspective is that empirical studies of externalization typically involve pressure – whether intentional or unintentional – related to the EU's market size and/or an individual or constellation of the actors operating within EU policy-making processes and rules, and/or coalitions of interest groups.

FURTHER REFLECTIONS ON POTENTIAL MPE CONTRIBUTIONS

In addition to its dynamic nature, MPE may offer empirical and methodological contributions that further our understanding of the EU as a power. This section sketches out such potential contributions, in particular the ways in which the subjects of MPE externalization may be empirically broadened and the MPE approach may be used to avoid methodological pitfalls related to evaluating policy inconsistency in EU external relations.

The EU is active – to varying degrees – in all policy areas on the international agenda. In empirical terms then, MPE needs to consider a wide variety of policy areas as well as the diverse non-EU public and private targets of externalization, such as 'states, international and regional organizations, and non-state actors' (Damro 2012: 690), that may be active in those policy areas. From an analytical point of view, the EU's wide range of targets and policy areas in its external relations also means that there is great potential for cross-policy analyses that may reveal insights into the fungibility of power. To capture this potential, the dynamic nature of MPE allows it to be more inclusive of policy areas than restrictive. The point of a conceptual framework is not to delineate exactly what the EU can and cannot externalize but to suggest ways forward in which the 'subjects' (Damro 2012: 690) that the EU externalizes can be interpreted in a broad enough way to capture empirical diversity across policy areas.

THE EUROPEAN UNION AS A GLOBAL REGULATOR?

The original formulation of MPE identified the 'subjects' of externalization as the EU's economic and social market-related policies and regulatory measures. These subjects of externalization are not limited to the narrow set of policies often associated directly with the internal market. Rather, they may be thought of as a range of the policies and measures the EU externalizes, running from directly market-related (e.g., competition policy, consumer policy) to indirectly market-related (e.g., environment, anti-discrimination, gender equality, protection of child). Within such a range, the subjects can also include private standards and soft law that are promoted by the EU. In addition, as noted above, because successful externalization may only result in other actors behaving in a way that *generally satisfies or conforms to* the EU's market-related policies and regulatory measures, the subjects may include internationally and bilaterally developed rules (Barbé *et al.* 2009) and internationally agreed objectives (Scott 2014) that are mirrored in – but not necessarily identical to – the EU's internal rules.

To illustrate the empirical basis of this broad and flexible interpretation of the subjects of externalization, we need only look to the EU's primary legislation, its treaties. Indeed, with the removal of the Maastricht pillar structure, conceptual lines of demarcation among different policies are less clear. For example, as Article 3(3) TEU clarifies, the internal market is related to a variety of policies, including, *inter alia*, areas traditionally thought of as the domain of other conceptualizations in the EU-as-a-power debates (e.g., human rights, sustainable development, gender equality, solidarity).[19] Broadening further, MPE's understanding of economic and social market-related policies and regulatory measures can be interpreted to cover all types of EU legislation and instruments (including those arising from private standard-setting bodies) and, conceivably, the entire *acquis*. When viewed in the context of enlargement policy, these subjects may even be conceived of as including the full set of Copenhagen criteria.

While there may be a relative absence of physical force in the EU's exercise of power (Damro 2012: 691), this does not mean that MPE cannot contribute to an understanding of the EU as a security actor. Indeed, under the broad interpretation of the subjects of externalization sketched herein, the potential for studying the fungibility of power is maximized because the conceptualization may be applied to market-related policies and regulatory measures that are associated with security, such as sanctions, arms trade and the defence industry.[20] The Commission has also noted the market-related link with security in its efforts toward an export control system for dual-use goods (European Commission 2010: 15). Such internal export control measures have serious security-related implications for the activities of others – including governments, firms and non-governmental actors – outside the EU seeking to import or (legally or otherwise) obtain European dual-use goods. Likewise, the EU's efforts towards a comprehensive approach (Gebhard 2013) may provide fruitful inroads for MPE analyses of more traditionally security-related policy areas like the Common Foreign and Security Policy and the Common Security and Defence Policy.

THE EUROPEAN UNION AS A GLOBAL REGULATOR?

Another way in which the MPE conceptualization may contribute to the EU-as-a-power debates is by helping to avoid methodological pitfalls related to evaluating policy inconsistency. While a number of scholars have identified different types of practical or policy inconsistency in EU external action, the discussion herein focuses upon what might be called 'internal' and 'horizontal' inconsistency within, between or among different policies (Gebhard 2011).[21] Such policy inconsistency is analytically problematic because it can create methodological pitfalls for the EU-as-a-power debates when EU objectives are broadly constructed as imprecise civilian ends, values, principles and/or norms.[22]

For example, starting at the origin of the EU-as-a-power debates and taking a civilian power perspective, the EU can be seen to pursue 'civilian ends' as its objectives (Orbie 2008). While there is disagreement over exactly what are these civilian ends, Smith (2005: 66) has noted that they tend to include goals such as international co-operation; solidarity; strengthening the rule of law; responsibility for the global environment; and diffusion of equality, justice and tolerance. While these goals may be normatively appealing, Smith (2005: 67) has argued that 'the problem here is that such civilian ends are still quite fuzzily defined (for example, what does "solidarity" mean in terms of policy practice?)'. As a result, 'not only do we not have a good idea of what "civilian ends" are, but also we cannot (and should not) state uncritically that the EU is actually pursuing civilian ends' (*ibid*: 74). In effect, because these civilian ends are 'fuzzily defined', they become analytically problematic insofar as their fuzzy nature means they can overlap or outright conflict.

From another prominent contribution to the EU-as-a-power debates, we learn that the EU's objectives can be thought of as norms. In his influential formulation of normative power Europe, Manners (2002) has argued for consideration of five core norms – peace, liberty, democracy, rule of law and respect for human rights and fundamental freedoms – and four minor norms – social solidarity, anti-discrimination, sustainable development and good governance. Again, the problem of policy inconsistency may arise when promoting such norms.[23] From a methodological point of view, the core of this problem is that any instance of externalization that appears to be the promotion of one fuzzily defined norm may at the same time contradict or be inconsistent with the promotion of other fuzzily defined norms. The resulting uncertainty about what exactly is being promoted and the inability to disentangle empirically what the EU is doing as a power leaves little room for scholars to generate with confidence any general statements about what kind of power the EU really is or to judge what the EU says and does as a power.

This methodological pitfall associated with policy inconsistency may be overcome with an MPE approach that encourages a more targeted analysis geared toward tracing the EU's externalisation of market-related policies and regulatory measures. In order to understand the EU as a power, MPE does not require the EU to be policy-consistent in its externalisation nor does it require the EU's objectives to be consistent. Rather, it provides a framework through which

THE EUROPEAN UNION AS A GLOBAL REGULATOR?

the EU's externalisation can be traced and evaluated without depending upon reference to rather vague and general objectives (i.e., higher-order ends and norms) that may contain multiple meanings and/or are inconsistent or inconsistently pursued in practice. Such an approach encourages analysis of the EU as a power through the careful and empirically detailed interrogation of the more specific and fine-grained (often technical) subjects of market-related policies and regulatory measures. By avoiding the methodological pitfall of inconsistency, the conceptual framework also usefully opens space for analysing the fungibility of power. Without doing so, it would be analytically problematic to separate and know when power in one policy area becomes power in another because exercises of power in each area under investigation may pull against the multiple and inconsistent meanings of fuzzily defined general objectives.

CONCLUSIONS

As a stock-taking exercise, this contribution has explored the utility of considering and employing market power Europe as a conceptual framework, an analytical tool that may help to advance our empirical and theoretical understanding of the EU as a power. While numerous other contributions offer ways in which to conceive of the EU as a power, the result is a rather fragmented and often descriptive literature, or set of debates, among seemingly rival conceptualizations. These debates tend to understand (at least implicitly) the EU as a unique or *sui generis* actor, which can limit the extent to which contributions benefit from and add to other more generalizable literatures. At the same time, contributions to the debates tend to emphasize ideational dynamics and the persuasive nature of the EU as a power while overlooking the potential roles played by various other factors that may arise from core characteristics of the EU's identity as a power.

When viewed as an explicit and dynamic conceptual framework, MPE may add considerable value to these debates. Given its generalizable foundations, the framework does not depend upon or advance an understanding of the EU being *sui generis*. Rather, by drawing from the CIPE literature, MPE's generalizable foundations – its three core characteristics – may be common to any market power's identity. This reliance on the broader and more general CIPE literature also helps to ensure that the framework is analytically flexible enough to take into account new theoretical and empirical developments arising from research on the material/interest-based *and* social/ideational sources of power.

As shown in recent research related to the conceptualization, the three characteristics of MPE can be thought of in a variety of ways. Through an MPE approach, the extent to which these three characteristics contribute to externalization of market-related policies and regulatory measures can be analysed in two stages. Across these two stages, investigations need to consider the role of persuasion and coercion as well as intentionality and unintentionality. But

THE EUROPEAN UNION AS A GLOBAL REGULATOR?

they also need to consider variation in EU attempts and non-attempts, as well as actual success and failure. Despite a tendency in the growing literature on the EU as an international regulator to see the EU as a dominant actor, MPE is flexible enough to accommodate the failure of externalization without losing its conceptual or analytical value. This flexibility also allows for and encourages further adjustment and revision of MPE as ongoing research continues to generate new findings that may help to elaborate more thoroughly and extensively the three characteristics and externalization, as well as additional external factors that may condition the EU's exercise of power.

These insights into the ways in which MPE may contribute to the EU-as-a-power debates also help to identify other important areas for further research efforts. For example, while MPE's focus on a wide variety of directly and indirectly market-related policies and regulatory measures expands the scope of analysis, it increases analytical precision by avoiding methodological pitfalls that may arise when evaluating the EU's pursuit of fuzzily defined and potentially inconsistent objectives. In particular, the approach encourages careful and empirically detailed interrogation of the EU's more specific and fine-grained subjects of externalization. In addition, the concept of externalization can, at least theoretically, be applied across all policy areas, which may provide important inroads for analysing the fungibility of the EU's power. Empirical work along such lines may even help to reveal the extent to which the framework can (or cannot) contribute to the analysis of power in more traditionally security-related policy areas. Ultimately, these reflections reveal the feasibility and benefits of employing MPE as a conceptual framework and suggest its potential for opening new exploratory avenues and contributing to theoretical developments in our understanding of the EU as an international regulator and, more generally, as a power.

Biographical note: Chad Damro is senior lecturer of politics and international relations and Co-Director of the Europa Institute at the University of Edinburgh.

ACKNOWLEDGMENTS

For useful comments, I would like to thank participants at the workshop on 'Regulatory power Europe? Assessing the EU's efforts to shape global rules', sponsored by the Jean Monnet Chair at the Georgia Institute of Technology (USA), 18–19 April 2014. This work also benefitted from a Fernand Braudel Senior Fellowship at the European University Institute in Florence, Italy (2013–14), particularly discussions with Ulrich Krotz and William Phelan. Special thanks to Alasdair Young for his encouragement and critical

THE EUROPEAN UNION AS A GLOBAL REGULATOR?

comments, as well as two anonymous reviewers for particularly useful comments.

NOTES

1 This understanding is also reflected in external perceptions of the EU (Chaban and Holland 2008; Larsen 2014; Lucarelli and Fioramonti 2009). Insofar as external perceptions matter for shaping an actor's identity, such findings are important for making claims about the appropriateness of how to conceptualize the EU as a power.

2 For more recent treatments of civilian power, see Orbie (2008), Smith (2005) and Telò (2005).

3 For a similar characterization of these contributions as 'debates', see Neimann and Bretherton (2013: 263).

4 For a significant research effort that draws from other literatures to examine the role of the EU as a promoter and recipient of ideas, see Börzel and Risse's 'Transformative power Europe' project at http://www.polsoz.fu-berlin.de/en/v/transformeurope/ (accessed 31 March 2015).

5 There are, however, efforts to link individual conceptualizations to explanatory theory. See, for example, Manners's (2013: 304) claim that the normative power *approach* 'makes it possible to explain, understand and judge the EU in global politics'.

6 In addition, for a discussion of EU relational and structural power, see Keukeleire and Delreux (2014). See also Hill and Smith (2011) for different perspectives on the EU's exercise of power.

7 See Meunier and Nicolaïdis (2006) for a discussion of the fungibility of EU trade power in the pursuit of non-trade objectives.

8 For exceptions that consider both ideational and material factors in the analysis of the EU as a power, see Youngs (2004) and contributions to Whitman (2011).

9 While Blaikie refers to 'conceptual schemes', his discussion of such analytical tools conforms to the understanding of 'conceptual frameworks' used herein.

10 For earlier discussions of market size from the CIPE literature, see Drezner (2007) and Gilpin (2001).

11 For examples, see Birchfield (2015); Jurje and Lavenex (2014); Miller *et al.* (2014); Oberthür and Rabitz (2014); Quaglia (2014a); Schulze and Tosun (2013); Staniland (2012); Turkina and Postnikov (2014); Young (2014).

12 For a discussion of the nature of the EU as a regulatory state in the context of the EU-as-a-power debates, see Orbie (2008: 27–30).

13 Such extensions can take place, for example, through technical assistance (Sabel and Zeitlin 2010: 22–3) or when third parties are included in the EU's internal governance processes across different policy areas (Lavenex 2014; Zeitlin 2015).

14 For examples of relevant CIPE work on domestic actors and preferences for externalizing product and process regulations, see Kelemen (2010), Kelemen and Vogel (2010) and Vogel (1995). For the different domestic bargaining dynamics at play in externalization, see Young and Wallace (2000) and Holzinger *et al.* (2008).

15 In addition, for a useful analysis of the EU's role in international institutions that hinges on a related concept of 'performance', see Oberthür *et al.* (2013).

16 Instead of attempting to externalize, the EU may also engage in what Müller *et al.* (2014) refer to as policy protection or policy import. While not attempts at externalization *per se*, they are important variations in EU global regulatory behaviour *vis-à-vis* international institutions. As such, it is worthy of investigating the extent to which market size, institutional features and interest contestation figure in the likelihood of the EU pursuing either of these two options.

THE EUROPEAN UNION AS A GLOBAL REGULATOR?

17 See also Young (2015) for a discussion of processes of policy diffusion in the context of EU regulatory relations.
18 For Holzinger and Knill, the absence of communication may lead to independent problem-solving, through which convergence arises 'as a result of similar but independent responses of political actors to parallel problem pressures' (2005: 786). Under such conditions, it is unclear that the three characteristics of MPE would play any role in independent problem-solving.
19 For Article 3(3), see http://www.lisbon-treaty.org/wcm/the-lisbon-treaty/treaty-on-european-union-and-comments/title-1-common-provisions/4-article-3.html (accessed 24 March 2015).
20 For an investigation of the relationship between the EU's arms industry/trade and its normative power rhetoric, see Erickson (2013).
21 For further discussions of consistency, see Keukeleire and Delreux (2014: 113–15) and Portela and Raube (2012).
22 For discussions of different analytical and methodological aspects and problems related to the issue of inconsistency and the EU-as-a-power debates, see Diez (2005, 2013), Whitman (2011), Scheipers and Sicurelli (2007), Meunier and Nicolaïdis (2006) and Sjursen (2006). For a useful analysis that reveals the ways in which seemingly complementary objectives may become conflicting objectives, see Börzel and van Hüllen (2014).
23 Manners (2011: 233) seems to agree when he argues that 'if normative justification is to be convincing or attractive, then the principles being promoted must be seen as legitimate, as well as being promoted in a coherent and consistent way'.

REFERENCES

Allen, D. and Smith, M. (1990) 'Western Europe's presence in the contemporary international arena', *Review of International Studies* 16(1): 19–37.
Bach, D. and Newman, A. (2007) 'The European regulatory state and global public policy: micro-institutions, macro-influence', *Journal of European Public Policy* 14(6): 827–46.
Barbé, E., Costa, O., Herranz Surrallés, A. and Natorski, M. (2009) 'Which rules shape EU external governance? Patterns of rule selection in foreign and security policies', *Journal of European Public Policy* 16(6): 834–52.
Barnett, M. and Duvall, R. (2005) 'Power in international politics', *International Organization* 59(1): 39–75.
Bicchi, F. (2006) 'Our size fits all: normative power Europe and the Mediterranean', *Journal of European Public Policy* 13(2): 286–303.
Birchfield, V. (2015) 'Coercion with kid gloves: the European Union's role in shaping a global regulatory framework for aviation emissions', *Journal of European Public Policy*, doi: 10.1080/13501763.2015.1046904.
Blaikie, N. (2000) *Designing Social Research*, Cambridge: Polity Press.
Bradford, A. (2012) 'The Brussels effect', *Northwestern University Law Review* 107(1): 1–68.
Bradford, A. (2014) 'Exporting standards: the externalization of the EU's regulatory power via markets', *International Review of Law and Economics*, doi: 10.1016/j.irle.2014.09.004.
Bretherton, C. and Vogler, J. (2005) *The European Union as a Global Actor*, 2nd ed., Abingdon: Routledge.
Börzel, T. and van Hüllen, V. (2014) 'One voice, one message, but conflicting goals: cohesiveness and consistency in the European Neighbourhood Policy', *Journal of European Public Policy* 21(7): 1033–49.

THE EUROPEAN UNION AS A GLOBAL REGULATOR?

Chaban, N. and Holland, M. (eds) (2008) *The European Union and the Asia–Pacific: Media, Public and Elite Perceptions of the EU*, London: Routledge.

da Conceição-Heldt, E. and Meunier, S. (2014) 'Speaking with a single voice: internal cohesiveness and external effectiveness of the EU in global governance', *Journal of European Public Policy* 21(7): 961–79.

Damro, C. (2012) 'Market power Europe', *Journal of European Public Policy* 19(5): 682–99.

Diez, T. (2005), 'Constructing the self and changing others: reconsidering "normative power Europe"', *Millennium* 33(3): 613–36.

Diez, T. (2013) 'Normative power as hegemony', *Cooperation and Conflict* 48(2): 194–210.

Diez, T., Stetter, S. and Albert, M. (2006) 'The European Union and border conflicts: the transformative power of integration', *International Organization* 60(3): 563–93.

Drezner, D. (2007) *All Politics is Global: Explaining International Regulatory Regimes*, Princeton, NJ: Princeton University Press.

Duchêne, F. (1972) 'Europe's role in world peace', in R. Mayne (ed.), *Europe Tomorrow*, London: Fontana, pp. 32–47.

Erickson, J.L. (2013) 'Market imperative meets normative power: human rights and European arms', *European Journal of International Relations* 19(2): 209–34.

European Commission (2010) 'Trade, growth and world affairs: trade policy as a core component of the EU's 2020 strategy', *COM(2010)612*, Brussels: Directorate General Trade, available at http://trade.ec.europa.eu/doclib/docs/2010/november/tradoc_146955.pdf (accessed 28 May 2015).

Forsberg, T. (2011) 'Normative power Europe, once again: a conceptual analysis of an ideal type', *Journal of Common Market Studies* 49(6): 1183–204.

Gebhard, C. (2011) 'Coherence', in C.Hill and Smith M. (eds), *International Relations and the European Union*, 2nd ed., Oxford: Oxford University Press, pp. 101–27.

Gebhard, C. (2013) 'A European approach to comprehensive security?', *European Foreign Affairs Review* 18(4): 1–6.

Gilpin, R. (2001) *Global Political Economy*, Princeton NJ: Princeton University Press.

Hill, C. and Smith, M. (eds) (2011) *International Relations and the European Union*, 2nd ed., Oxford: Oxford University Press.

Holden, P. (2009) *In Search of Structural Power: EU Aid Policy as a Global Political Instrument*, Farnham: Ashgate.

Holzinger, K. and Knill, C. (2005) 'Causes and conditions of cross-national policy convergence', *Journal of European Public Policy* 12(5): 775–96.

Holzinger, K., Knill, C. and Sommerer, T. (2008) 'Environmental policy convergence: the impact of international harmonization, transnational communication and regulatory competition', *International Organization* 62(4): 553–87.

Hyde-Price, A. (2006) 'Normative' power Europe: a realist critique', *Journal of European Public Policy* 13(2): 217–34.

Jurje, F. and Lavenex, S. (2014) 'Trade agreements as venues for "market power Europe"? The case of immigration policy', *Journal of Common Market Studies* 52(2): 320–36.

Kelemen, D. (2010) 'Globalizing European Union environmental policy', *Journal of European Public Policy* 17(3): 335–49.

Kelemen, D. and Vogel, D. (2010) 'Trading places: the role of the United States and the European Union in international environmental politics', *Comparative Political Studies* 43(4): 427–56.

Keukeleire, S. and Delreux, T. (2014) *The Foreign Policy of the European Union*, 2nd ed., Basingstoke: Palgrave.

Kissack, R. (2015) 'Man overboard!' Was EU influence on the Maritime Labour Convention lost at sea?', *Journal of European Public Policy*, doi: 10.1080/13501763.2015. 1046899.

THE EUROPEAN UNION AS A GLOBAL REGULATOR?

Larsen, H. (2014) 'The EU as a normative power and the research on external perceptions: the missing link', *Journal of Common Market Studies* 52(4): 896–910.

Lavenex, S. (2014) 'The power of functionalist extension: how EU rules travel', *Journal of European Public Policy* 21(6): 885–903.

Lucarella, S. and Fioramonti, L. (eds) (2009) *External Perceptions of the European Union as a Global Actor*, London: Routledge.

Majone, G. (1994) 'The rise of the regulatory state in Europe', *West European Politics* 17(3): 77–101.

Majone, G. (1997) 'From the positive to the regulatory state', *Journal of Public Policy* 17(2): 139–67.

Manners, I. (2002) 'Normative power Europe: a contradiction in terms?', *Journal of Common Market Studies* 40(2): 235–58.

Manners, I. (2011) 'The European Union's normative power: critical perspectives and perspectives on the critical', in R. Whitman (ed.), *Normative Power Europe: Empirical and Theoretical Perspectives*, Basingstoke: Palgrave Macmillan, pp. 226–47.

Manners, I. (2013) 'Assessing the decennial, reassessing the global: understanding European Union normative power in global politics', *Cooperation and Conflict* 48(2): 304–29.

Meunier, S. and Nicolaïdis, K. (2006) 'The European Union as a conflicted trade power', *Journal of European Public Policy* 13(6): 906–25.

Miller, A.M.M., Bush, S.R. and Mol, A.P.J. (2014) 'Power Europe: EU and the illegal, unreported and unregulated tuna fisheries regulation in the West and Central Pacific Ocean', *Marine Policy* 45: 138–45.

Müller, P., Kudrna, Z. and Falkner, G. (2014) 'EU–global interactions: policy export, import, promotion and protection', *Journal of European Public Policy* 21(8): 1102–19.

Newman, A.L. and Posner, E. (2015) 'Putting the EU in its place: policy strategies and the global regulatory context', *Journal of European Public Policy*, doi: 10.1080/13501763.2015.1046901.

Nicolaïdis, K. and Howse, R. (2003) '"This is my EUtopia … ": narrative as power', in J.H.H.Weiler, I. Begg and J. Peterson (eds), *Integration in an Expanding EU*, Oxford: Blackwell, pp. 341–66.

Niemann, A. and Bretherton, C. (2013) 'EU external policy at the crossroads: the challenge of actorness and effectiveness', *International Relations* 27(3): 261–75.

Oberthür, S., Jorgensen, K.E. and Shahin, J. (eds) (2013) *The Performance of the EU in International Institutions*, Abingdon: Routledge.

Oberthur, S. and Rabitz, F. (2014) 'On the EU's performance and leadership in global environmental governance: the case of the Nagoya Protocol', *Journal of European Public Policy* 21(1): 39–57.

Orbie, J. (ed.) (2008) *Europe's Global Role: External Policies of the European Union*, Farnham: Ashgate.

Phelan, W. (2012) 'What is *sui generis* about the European Union? Costly international cooperation in a self-contained regime', *International Studies Review* 14(3): 367–85.

Pollack, M.A. (2012) 'Living in a material world: a critique of "normative power Europe"', in H. Zimmermann and A. Dür (eds), *Key Controversies in European Integration*, Basingstoke: Palgrave Macmillan, pp. 199–205.

Portela, C., and Raube, K. (2012), 'The EU polity and foreign policy coherence', *Journal of Contemporary European Research* 8(1): 3–20.

Postnikov, E. and Bastiaens, I. (2014), 'Does dialogue work? The effectiveness of labor standards in EU preferential trade agreements', *Journal of European Public Policy* 21(6): 923–40.

Quaglia, L. (2014a) 'The sources of European Union influence in international financial regulatory fora, *Journal of European Public Policy* 21(3): 327–45.

THE EUROPEAN UNION AS A GLOBAL REGULATOR?

Quaglia, L. (2014b) 'The European Union, the USA and international standard setting in finance', *New Political Economy* 19(3): 427–44.

Ravitch, S.M. and Riggan, M. (2012) *Reason and Rigor: How Conceptual Frameworks Guide Research*, Thousand Oaks, CA: Sage.

Rosamond, B. (2005) 'Conceptualizing the EU model of governance in world politics', *European Foreign Affairs Review* 10(4): 463–78.

Sabel, C.F. and Zeitlin, J. (eds) (2010) *Experimentalist Governance in the European Union: Towards a New Architecture*, Oxford: Oxford University Press.

Scheipers, S. and Sicurelli, D. (2007) 'Normative power Europe: a credible utopia?', *Journal of Common Market Studies* 45(2): 435–57.

Schulze, K. and Tosun, J. (2013) 'External dimensions of European environmental policy: an analysis of environmental treaty ratification by third states', *European Journal of Political Research* 52(5): 581–607.

Scott, J. (2014) 'Extraterritoriality and territorial extension in EU Law' *American Journal of Comparative Law* 62(1): 87–126.

Shields, P. and Rangarajan, N. (2013) *A Playbook for Research Methods: Integrating Conceptual Frameworks and Project Management*, Stillwater, OK: New Forums Press.

Sjursen, H. (2006) 'The EU as a "normative" power: how can this be?', *Journal of European Public Policy* 13(2): 235–51.

Smith, K.E. (2005) 'Beyond the civilian power debate', available at: http://eprints.lse.ac.uk/812 (accessed 28 May 2015).

Staniland, M. (2012) 'Regulating aircraft emissions: leadership and market power', *Journal of European Public Policy* 19(7): 1006–25.

Telò, M. (2005) *Europe: A Civilian Power?* Basingstoke: Palgrave Macmillan.

Turkina, E. and Postnikov, E. (2014) 'From business to politics: cross-border inter-firm networks and policy spillovers in the EU's eastern neighbourhood', *Journal of Common Market Studies* 52(5): 1120–41.

Vogel, D. (1995) *Trading Up: Consumer and Environmental Regulation in the Global Economy*, Cambridge, MA: Harvard University Press.

Whitman, R. (ed.) (2011) *Normative Power Europe: Empirical and Theoretical Perspectives*, Basingstoke: Palgrave Macmillan.

Young, A. (2015) 'The European Union as a global regulator? Context and comparison', *Journal of European Public Policy*, doi: 10.1080/13501763.2015.1046902.

Young, A.R. (2014) 'Europe as a global regulator? The limits of EU influence in international food safety standards', *Journal of European Public Policy* 21(6): 904–22.

Young, A.R. and Wallace H. (2000) *Regulatory Politics in the Enlarging European Union: Weighing Civic and Producer Interests*, Manchester: Manchester University Press.

Youngs, R. (2004) 'Normative dynamics and strategic interests in the EU's external identity', *Journal of Common Market Studies* 42(2): 415–35.

Zeitlin, J. (ed.) (2015) *Extending Experimentalist Governance? The European Union and Transnational Regulation*, Oxford: Oxford University Press.

Zielonka, J. (2011) 'The EU as an international actor: unique or ordinary?', *European Foreign Affairs Review* 16(3): 281–301.

Zimmermann, H. (2007) 'Realist power Europe?', *Journal of Common Market Studies* 45(4): 813–32.

Index

accounting standards 96–97
adjustment costs 10, 26, 88
agenda-setting 13, 86, 94–95
airline industry 55–56
Air Transport Association (ATA) 55
Association of European Airlines (AEA) 58
aviations emissions 12–15, 44–59, 111

bargaining power 9–11, 15, 27
better alternative to negotiated agreement (BATNA) 9
bilateral trade agreements 21–23, 37
Brussels effect 87

Canada 22, 28, 31, 32
cap and trade system 47, 52; *see also* Emissions Trading System (ETS)
Central America 16, 22, 28, 29, 31, 32, 33, 34, 38
Central Europe 88
Chicago Convention 49, 54
Chile 23
China 47, 54
civilian ends 115
civilian power 87–89, 99
climate change 10, 44–59
coalition-building 86, 97–99
Codex Alimentarius 98, 99
coercion 16, 45, 56–59, 88–89
cohesiveness 9
Committee on Aviation Environmental Protection (CAEP) 50, 52
comparative and international political economy (CIPE) 104
comparative politics 86
competition policy 22, 32–33
Comprehensive Economic and Trade Agreement (CETA) 28, 31
conceptual frameworks 107–9

convergence; *see* regulatory convergence
Copenhagen United Nations Climate Conference 45, 46, 48–49

data protection 22, 29, 33
Decent Work campaign 68
dispute resolution 30, 31
domestic actors 111

Eastern Europe 88
Emissions Trading System (ETS) 12, 15, 45, 46, 47, 50–59
enforcement capacity 9–10
environmental agreements 3, 16
environmental protection 22, 29, 34, 37; aviations emissions and 12–15, 44–59, 111
equivalence 25, 27, 38–39
European Commission (EC) 22, 56, 58
European Court of Justice (ECJ) 70
European Economic Community (EEC) 69
European Union (EU): aviations emissions and 12–15, 44–59, 111; EU-as-a-power debates and 105–7, 114–15, 117; external policy strategies 2; global regulatory context and 84–100; ILO and 69–71; international presence of 3; labour standards and 3, 5, 13, 22, 29, 34, 37, 63–80; market size 9–11, 46, 91, 109–10; as normative power 3, 16, 45–46, 57–58, 87–88, 99, 115; policy strategies of 92–94; preferential trade agreements by 2, 11–16, 21–40; regulatory co-ordination by 28–34; as regulatory hegemon 87–89; regulatory power of 1–17, 21–22, 63–69; as regulatory state 110; as security actor 114; as *sui generis* 106–7, 116
exclusion 9, 11–13, 15, 22, 26, 27, 59
experimentalist governance 110
externalization 111, 112–13´

123

INDEX

financial services 9–10, 22, 32, 37
firm behaviour 4, 5, 6
first-mover agenda setting 2, 86, 94–95
food safety 31

Global Europe strategy 22, 23, 28
globalization 87, 91
global regulatory context 84–100, 111
goal attainment 3
goods, trade in 30–31
government effectiveness 28
greenhouse gas emissions 44–59
Group on International Aviation and
    Climate Change (GIACC) 52

harmonization; *see* regulatory harmonization
High-Level Meeting on International
    Aviation and Climate Change 52, 53
human rights 16

India 47
influence; *see* regulatory influence
institutional density 91–94
interdependence 99
interest contestation 111
internal market 114
international agreements 111
International Air Transport Association
    (IATA) 54, 55
International Civil Aviation Organization
    (ICAO) 13, 15, 44–46, 49–56, 58
International Convention for the
    Prevention of Pollution from Ships
    (MARPOL) 64
International Convention for the Safety of
    Lives at Sea (SOLAS) 64
International Convention on Standards of
    Training, Certification and Watchkeeping
    (STCW) 64
International Financial Reporting Standards
    (IFRS) 96–97
international institutionalization 95
International Labour Organization (ILO)
    5, 15, 63, 64, 66–80
International Maritime Organization
    (IMO) 64
international negotiations 3
International Panel on Climate Change
    (IPCC) 50
international relations 3, 10, 86, 105–6

international standards 4–6, 24–25, 30, 36,
    85, 87–88, 99
international standard-setting bodies
    10–11
International Standards Organization (ISO)
    95, 99

Kyoto Protocol 44, 46–51, 54
labour standards 3, 5, 13, 22, 29, 34, 37,
    63–80

Lisbon Treaty 48

Maritime Labor Convention (MLC)
    2, 11–15, 16, 63–80; amendment
    procedure 73–74; EU influence on
    72–80; inspection and enforcement
    74–75; negotiations timeline 77–78;
    scope of 75–76; social security and 76;
    structure of 72–73
market access 9–10
market-based measures (MBMs) 52, 53
market power Europe (MPE) 2, 16, 45–46,
    57–58, 87, 90–91, 104–17; characteristics
    of 109–11; as conceptual framework
    105, 107–9; EU-as-a-power debates and
    105–7, 114–15, 117; externalization
    and 112–13; new research findings
    and 109–13; potential contributions of
    113–16
market rules 84
market size 10–11, 26, 27, 46, 91, 109–10
Mexico 23
motor vehicles 30–31
multilateral agreements 5, 6, 21, 30
multinational corporations (MNCs) 65
mutual recognition 2, 27, 29, 86, 88–89,
    96–97

N = 1 problem 106
neoliberal policies 68, 98
Netherlands 71
normative power 3, 16, 45–46, 57–58,
    87–89, 99, 115

observational equivalence 36

peer reviews 89
phytosanitary measures 22
policy diffusion 7, 8

INDEX

policy inconsistency 115
political economy 16–17, 87, 104
power-based bargaining 2, 9–13, 15, 22, 27
power resources 26
preferential trade agreements 2, 11–16, 21–40
product standards 29

reciprocal equivalence 27, 29, 38
regional economic integration organization (REIO) 65
regulatory capacity 11, 15, 17, 26–28, 85–86, 90–91, 93, 99, 110
regulatory competition 1–4, 8
regulatory context; *see* global regulatory context
regulatory convergence 24–25, 27, 34
regulatory co-operation 1–3, 7–12, 15, 22, 88–89, 92; vs. diffusion 69; explanation of 25–27
regulatory co-ordination: assessment of 29–30; competition policy 32–33; on data protection 33; on environmental protection 34; EU practice of 28–34; on financial services 32; forms of 24–25; on goods 30–31; on labour standards 34; limits of 34–38
regulatory diffusion 69
regulatory disputes 84
regulatory export 29, 34, 36, 86, 94
regulatory harmonization 22–26, 34, 37–38
regulatory hegemony 87–89
regulatory influence: operationalization of 4–7; variance in 7, 12–13, 15
regulatory interaction 2, 7–11
regulatory power: of EU 1–17, 21–22, 63–69; relative 15–16; resources 1, 3, 7–11; US 30–31, 87, 91
relative power 11
relative preferences 11
rule export 29, 34, 36, 86, 94
rule-mediated negotiation 2, 10–12, 65
rule stringency 26, 27

Sanitary and Phytosanitary (SPS) agreement 30
sanitary measures 22
Security and Exchange Commission (SEC) 96
security-related policies 114
Singapore 22, 28, 29, 31, 32, 33, 34
Single European Act 69–70

social security 76
social-trade nexus 68
South Africa 23, 28
South Korea 22, 30–31, 33, 34
state behaviour 4–5, 6
status quo 10, 12, 39, 88, 98
Stop the Clock initiative 53, 58
sustainable development 16

technical barriers to trade 22, 23–24, 30–31
Technical Barriers to Trade (TBA) agreement 30
territorial extension 9–10
theoretical frameworks 108
trade agreements; *see* preferential trade agreements
trade barriers 22–24, 30–31
trade liberalization 25, 29, 39
trade policy 22–24; *see also* preferential trade agreements
transaction costs 88
Transatlantic Trade and Investment Partnership (TTIP) 28, 37, 38
transnational coalitions 89

UN Climate Conference 45
unilateral equivalence 27, 38–39
unilateralism 56–57, 58
United Kingdom 71
United Nation's Economic Commission for Europe (UNECE) 30–31
United Nations Framework Convention on Climate Change (UNFCC) 45–47
United States 16; accounting standards 96–97; aviations emissions and 54–56; decentralized regulatory process in 95; EU negotiations with 22, 28, 29, 34, 37; Kyoto Protocol and 47; regulatory power of 17, 87, 91
US airline industry 55–56
US Generally Accepted Accounting Principles (USGAAP) 96–97

veterinary equivalence agreements (VEAs) 31

Washington Consensus 98
working conditions 68
World Trade Organization (WTO) 68, 84, 92